THE PRISON PHILOSOPHER

BAJAH OGINGA LANGLEY

THE PRISON PHILOSOPHER

BAJAH OGINGA LANGLEY

Cover Design By: Dynasty Visionary Designs
Facebook: facebook.com/dynastys.coverme
Email: covermeservice@yahoo.com

CONTENTS

INTRODUCTION
Penal Psychology 101

In case you want to know about prison…
Well, prison is nescience in psychological quicksand.

Where cavemen mentalities are arrested without development.

Loud voices resonating out of sync chirping lah, lah, lah.

A congregation of misconducts branded criminal elements.

Penal institutions are a place where premeditational psychosis as disguised as reform.

Strait–jacketed excursions marching disorder within a hemmed in sulky threshold… The election of psychosis bouncing off the walls multiplying collective unpleasant mirages.

Security guards are zoological employees feeding buffoonery with unrehabilitated policies.

Welcome to the Class of Penal Psychology 101

Doing time psychosocial skid marks deflates the cerebellum.

The opticals blink repulsively from artificial electromagnetic radiation.

Social pollution pollinates in a derelict population like Covid – 19.

Sadism fly high as smut repetitively hammers the cerebral cortex.

Gawkers are stouted in rigmarole.

Mental rigor mortis produces mental dehydration.
Comatose for a second and callousness greets you with an
insatiable slap. Smack! Ows, silhouettes into insidious howls.

As foul thoughts ascend and stick to the prison's ceiling.

Welcome to the Chamber of Penal Psychology 101

In the class of imprisonment necrophilia is the curriculum here.

The highest grade of savagery inaugurates you as valedictorian
here.

Graduation is decided by the highest effort of immorality here.

Peer pressure won't allow you to become independent without a
fight here.

Shadiness has an unconventional rule here united to keep human
bodies as commodities here,

Mainly to feed an underprivileged police force who is a class in
society of indentured servants and social remote-controlled
precisions for capitalism and fascism.

Badges of symbolisms taking oaths to uphold the destruction of
positive mental absorption.

Welcome to the Graduation of Penal Psychology 101
A school where ignobility earns a certificate.

Part One

The Prison Philosopher

The Dialogue:
"What Time Is It?!"

THE DIALOGUE: WHAT TIME IS IT?! PART ONE

An announcement is made over the prison's PA system:

"Attention Gray Unit… Attention on Gray Unit… The yard is open… The yard is now open! All Inmates have 5 minutes to report to the yard!"

Brothaman heads to the yard and begins his workout when he is approached by ignorance.

Streetz: "Yo, my nigga… What time is it?!

Brothaman: "Young Brotha… Are you talking to me?"

Streetz: "Yeah my nigga… I'm talkin' to you!"

Brothaman: "Well, my Brotha… If you really want to know the time… It's time to wake up! Brothaman was being sarcastic because of the way he was approached by Streetz.

Streetz: "Man, what da phuck you talkin' 'bout… It's time to wake up and shit! My nigga, I am awake!"

Brothaman: "Angu kaka, are you sure you are awake?!"

Streetz: "Yeah my nigga… I'm awake and what da phuck is an angu kaka anyway?!"

Brothaman: "Angu kaka means, 'My Brother' in Swahili."

Streetz: "My nigga I ain't yo brotha a'ight!"

Brothman: "If you weren't asleep young Brotha then you would overstand that you and I are indeed Brotha's."

Streetz: "Phuck ya mean…we don't have the same mother or father?!"

Brothaman: "Yet, we have the same genetic colors right?!"

Streetz: "Yeah! But that don't mean shit my nigga!"

Brothaman: "It actually means a lot. For one, it means that you and I come from the same root or from a common ancestry who are descendants of Alkebulan…"

Streetz: "Alkebulan?"

Brothaman: "Afrika… The original name our ancestors called this great continent we come from."

Streetz: "Ain't from no Alkebulan or Afrika my nigga. I was born right here in Amerika and so is my people, my family. Phuck ya mean we from Afrika?!"

Brothaman: "So, you think that you are Amerikan, huh?"

Streetz: "Yeah, my nigga… I'm Amerikan!"

Brothaman: "Ok. What exactly makes you an Amerikan my Brotha?"

Streetz: "I'm an Amerikan because I was born here… that's why!"

Brothaman: "Ok, so being born in Amerika makes you a citizen of this country… but what makes you an Amerikan my Brotha?"

Streetz: "Yeah, that's right my nigga!"

Brothaman: "And yet you are a slave."

Streetz: "I ain't no muthaphuckin' slave my nigga!"

Brothaman: "Is that so?"

Streetz: "Yeah my nigga… I ain't no slave!"

Brothaman: "Then how come you talk like one?"

Streetz: "What?!"

Brothaman: "You talk like a slave. A person that doesn't know their original language. We all do. The language we use and speak, the English language, is a European method of communication forced on us after they enslaved some of our ancestors in Amerika. The first thing the European colonizers did once some of our ancestors were enslaved was eradicating our native tongues, the way we naturally communicated. Stripping us from our natural languages divided us because it made us "forget" who and what we are. Basically, stripping us from our language. They whitewashed our memory to the point where we forgot who we were, our relationship to one another, and our nature. Therefore, it was easier to enslave us when our original tongue or language was eradicated and replaced with the English form. When a slave doesn't have a language of their own they will not think, perceive, or feel on their own because language is a way of life, culture, principle, and communication that reflects the way you think, create, grow and evolve."

Streetz: "But, I think just fine my nigga…."

Brothaman: "Yet, you can't perceive or feel that you and I are Brotha's? You can't perceive that we are brotha's because we don't speak the same language. Not being able to speak the same language in our original way of communicating, and speaking a foreign language, places us in a position where we won't recognize a natural relation to our own people. Instead, speaking a foreign language, rearranges and changes our perception and confuses the relation to our own people. It makes you think and feel like you are more related to the foreigner. The foreigner controls you through language."

Streetz: How can you say that we don't speak the same language when we both are speaking in English right now?!"

Brothaman: "We don't speak standard nor proper English… the language that makes us an Amerikan. Again, we aren't natural English people and we speak what you may call – Ebonics, which real English speakers call broken English. This means our relation to one another is disconnected and our communication, thinking, and perception, are not cohesive. It will stay fragmented as long as our communication, thinking, and perception is broken."

"We can be no more than slaves to the English way of thinking and perceiving, which is holistic or collectivist in nature. It makes us dependent on them in thinking and how things are perceived through English-speaking eyes."

"Speaking ebonics or even learning how to speak standard or proper English commands you to see and feel how English speaking people direct and dominate from their perspectives. Not to mention the fact how speaking ebonics or broken English places us in a position where ebonics speakers can only respond to those who command the English language, and they are no more than slave masters."

"Speaking the English language, whether ebonics, standard or proper, makes us respond to the English language like a dog recognizing his or her master's voice or sound. Language is important my Brotha. We can never be an Amerikan speaking ebonics, standard, or proper English. We can't because we aren't English people."

Streetz: (silent)

Brothaman continues: "Listen Bruh. The English language is a soulless language, meaning it has no rhythm. A language without rhythm is a language without feeling and creativity. Everything is created through rhythm and without rhythm, whoever is created becomes a clone. The English language is a cloned language. Cloned form languages that have rhythm. But, anything not original is the opposite. It is something artificial, which is not natural."

"Anything not natural is uncivilized and all illegitimate. Anything uncivilized and illegitimate brings chaos and confusion, which the English language does because the English language is a language attempting to be original by stealing from different sounds of rhythmical languages. It's a cloned language trying to sound and pass as original. While the English language can copy the sounds of rhythmical languages, there is one thing the English vowel sounds can't successfully do… copy rhythmical vowels because rhythm can't be cloned."

Brothaman continues: "If you ever heard and listen to an Afrikan speak, you can see, hear and feel the soul or rhythm. Naturally, we pronounce our vowels differently. For example, 'A' sounds like 'Ah and E' sounds like 'Eh'. 'I' sounds like 'EE' in see. 'O' has a long 'O' sound and 'U' sounds like 'OO' in the tooth. You try it. Sound out the vowels in the Afrikan way and take notice of how the sound vibrates and then sound out the vowels in English."

Streetz: (He pronounces the vowels the Afrikan way, then he pronounced the vowels the English way… a, e, I, o, u).

Brothman: "Can you hear and feel the difference the rhythm and vibration in the Afrikan way versus no rhythm and low vibration in the English way?"

Streetz: "Yeah!"

Brothaman: "It's the soul you hear and feel in the Afrikan way which is always holistic having healing effects. Our languages (tongues), connected to our true nature is extremely apparent and creative. Why do you think they say Black people have soul?"

Streetz: Because we have rhythm and are so creative?"

Brothaman: "Right! No matter what we go through, whatever situations or conditions, if we tap into our souls and find our rhythm, then we live in the creative process of the rhythm making us creators. Language is an important medium that helps free us from slavery and put us on the path of being conscious creators, creating and having control over our own destinies. Also, language is like a plug that plugs us into either a high or low frequency. The higher the frequency the better the creativity you can tune into control and direct at will. This is why English-speaking people don't want us speaking our native tongues using rhythmical sounds. Our language is like the sun… it's a higher energy frequency that vibrates and creates through rhythm."

"Rhythm is not artificial, chaotic, or confusing. Rhythm is a unitary principle, a harmonizing cause, and effect, a call and response. Everything in nature grows and evolves due to the vibrations of rhythm. We cannot grow, nor evolve, using the English language because it's a low frequency causing chaos, confusion, and division."

"And another point that proves we are slaves can be seen through our present condition…being incarcerated."

Streetz: "How is being in prison making me a slave man?!"

Brothaman: "Are you familiar with the United States Constitution, the amendment part?"

Streetz: "Not really my nigga."

Brothaman: "Well, the 13th amendment in the U.S. Constitution states neither slavery nor involuntary servitude, except as a punishment for a crime where if the party shall have been duly convicted..."

Streetz: "Hold up... that shit ya talkin' about sounds crazy yo!"

Brothaman: "Well, it's not! This is actually a law encoded in the U.S. Constitution in their language. It's even encoded into all the state constitutions no matter the state you were born in. So you see, just being convicted of a crime by them makes you, and everyone you know that has been convicted of a crime, a non-U.S. citizen. Also, they are telling us in a subtle way that we can not be a citizen in Amerika because citizens in Amerika are sovereigns, the convicted are not. Not being a sovereign means that you have no government and or nation."

"Therefore, you can never be a citizen as a dependent person or people like those convicted. Simply not having and using your own language proves that a person, or people, aren't independent because independent nations have their own languages and governments, but only use the English language to conduct business in English-speaking countries. So, do you still think you are a citizen in this country or some Amerikan?"

Streetz: "Yeah my nigga, I still believe I am an amerikan."

Brothaman: "Alright, can you vote my Brotha?"

Streetz: "No, but..."

Brothaman: "Why not?!"

Streetz: "My nigga you know we can't vote because we are in prison!"

Brothaman: "But if you are a citizen in this country you can't be disfranchised..." (Streetz cuts Brothaman off)

Streetz: "Disfranchise?"

Brothaman: "Disfranchise means that your right to vote has been deprived or denied. As a citizen, you can't be disfranchised or deprived from voting, even if you are in prison or have been to prison. In fact, the fifteenth amendment in the U.S. Constitution Section 1, explicitly states, '*The right of citizens of the United States to vote shall not be denied or abridged by the United States or by any state on account of race, color, or previous condition of servitude*'. Did you hear that last part? Remember the thirteenth amendment and what it says about slavery if you are convicted? See the contradiction in the English language? They are telling you that you can't be a citizen if you are convicted of a crime (13th amendment), and your right as a citizen to vote can't be taken away or violated because of the previous condition of servitude (15th amendment)."

Streetz: "Yo that's crazy Bro! But I still am an Amerikan cause I was born here."

Brothaman: "What is your government name if you don't mind me asking?"

Streetz: "What da phuck my name gotta do with anything?"

Brothaman: "Your name will prove if you are a slave or a free person in this country."

Streetz: "You ain't making no sense to me my nigga!"

Brothaman: "I can be clearer if you tell me your government name."

Streetz: "My government name is Toby Whitehead."

Brothaman: (laughs) "You ever seen Alex Haley's mini T.V. series or read his book called Roots?"

Streetz: "Nah man… and what's so funny about my name yo?"

Brothaman: "Well, Alex Haley's mini-series and book called Roots were about Mr. Haley tracing his ancestral Roots starting in Afrika, but ended up with one of his ancestors being kidnapped and enslaved in Amerika."

Brothaman continues: "Alex Haley traced his Roots to an Afrikan named Kunta Kinte who refused to be a slave in Amerika until they broke him. Kunta was forever trying to escape in order to go back home to Afrika, but didn't know this country here, so he was always caught and whipped. At first, Kunta refused to give up his ancestral language, because giving up his language meant losing his identity."

"Therefore, they constantly beat him for refusing to give up his language, and for escaping. Kunta could never understand why he was surrounded by others that looked like him, but had strange names and couldn't speak like him. He could never understand why they didn't fight to be free from the conditions of slavery. Kunta just couldn't understand these strange people that looked like him, but didn't sound like him and seemed content being slaves to the Wazungu (white people)."

Brothman continues: "Nevertheless, the slave master and a slave driver continuously tried to break Kunta because he kept trying to escape and wouldn't give up speaking in his native tongue. So, the slave master figured out that he had to get Kunta to give up his name and accept a name the slave master chose for him."

"After the slave master understood that he could break Kunta if he got Kunta to give up his name, Kunta Kinte was whooped so badly that he finally gave up his original name, Kunta Kinte, and accepted the name the slave master gave him. Kunta Kinte's new name became Toby! When Kunta accepted the name Toby, Kunta was broken and 99% of the rebellious attitude left him. Then, Kunta became a slave."

Brothaman continues: Mr. White…head. Think about it. Your last name is Whitehead. Anyway, you don't look like a Toby Whitehead to me. Your name doesn't sound Afrikan at all."

Streetz: "I told ya… I ain't Afrikan!"

Brothman: "You aren't European either, but you have two European names. So tell me, what does Toby Whitehead mean?"

Streetz: How da phuck I suppose to know that?!"

Brothaman: "The same way you figure you are an Amerikan."

Streetz: "My mother gave me that name and I never thought about it!"

Brothaman: "Not seeing the importance or relevance in something as a name, keeps us thinking, acting, speaking and labeled, as slaves, plus treated as such."

Streetz: "My nigga, it's just a name. (Streetz laughs). Man, you are on some other shit!"

Brothaman: "Having European names tell the whole world that we are slaves to the European race. That we are docile and still trapped in a comatose state of being ranked just a little higher than domesticated animals."

Streetz: "Man, what da hell you talkin' bout my nigga?!"

Brothaman: "A name reveals and allows you to express who you are, the way you think and perceive, your character, personality, and purpose. Not knowing these things about yourself makes you vulnerable and perpetual prey for free people in this country and abroad. A name defines and clarifies your true identity and exposes a false one if it doesn't reflect internally, nor verbally, your true identity."

Streetz: "Brothaman, you living in the past. We ain't in slavery no mo! The people that enslaved our people in the past are dead and gone."

Brothaman: "But their descendants are alive and have been trained or programmed to continue their ancestor's system of our enslavement consciously and unconsciously."

"The first wave of enslavers of our people are long dead, but their system is not. How to enslave or keep our people enslaved is encoded in every facet within their culture, language, religions, laws, business practices, and schools. Every English descendant in Amerika is subliminally or directly taught how to enslave or keep people labeled as minorities in this country enslaved to them. Their system gets more subtle, evolving in every generation. This is the Amerikan way or system. This is how English descendants stay in power and domination in each generation."

Brothaman continues: "What I am trying to get you to understand is we as a people, can never be Amerikan's unless we come from under the label of being labeled as minorities (a subtle way of labeling us slaves), and become sovereignty. We as a people are still slaves in this country and in any country under a system or program not indigenous for us. We as a people, have to either change those systems and programs that have kept us bound to enslavement for four hundred and two years now. And the only way to do that is by returning to our natural habitat or indigenous way of 'Being', starting spiritually, mentally, and culturally. We achieve our freedom when we return to our Roots and become sovereign. This can be done no matter where we are. But first, we have to wake up!"

Streetz: (laughs) "There you go with that wake-up shit again, my nigga!" (still laughing) "Man, you just ain't making no kind of sense to me and you sound like a racist, yo!"

Brothaman: "Listen. I'm not a racist. I'm race-conscious! How else am I supposed to be when they label me 3/5 of a man. It's right there still hanging in their constitution. The way they treat me giving them the legal right to shoot me for sport or put me further into slavery, but I am the racist you say?! I'm not a racist, I'm race-conscious!"

"For listening to my ancestor's voices, I'm supposed to be a racist?! For revolting against injustice, I'm supposed to be a racist?! For speaking about systemic racism in Amerika, I'm supposed to be a racist?! For loving my Beautiful Black women, I'm supposed to be a racist?! Oh, for teaching Black children to appreciate their history, I'm supposed to be a racist?! I'm not a racist, I'm race-conscious!"

"You say I am a racist because I buy and support Black Arts?! You say I am a racist because I say God is not blue-eyed and blond?! You say I am a racist because I like to wear Kinte cloth?! You say I am a racist because I rather go to Ethiopia instead of London? You say I am a racist because I let my dreadlocks grow the roots of the Afro?! I'm not a racist, I'm race-conscious!"

"I've been called a racist for not wearing a suit and tie. I've been called a racist for not speaking proper English. I've been branded a racist for saying, Black Lives Matter. I've been said to be a racist for protesting police shootings. I've been told I am a racist for burning the confederate stars and bars. I'm not a racist, I'm race-conscious!"

"I'm a racist for wanting equality, right?! I'm a racist for refusing to entertain white folks like sambos right?! I'm racist for sayin' Jesus was really a Black man named Yahoshua, right? I'm racist for worshipping Malcolm X as my hero right?! I guess I am a racist for waving the Red, Gold, Green, and Black Flag, right? Nah, I'm not a racist, I'm race-conscious!"

Streetz: "Ok, how we goin' to be slaves when Abraham Lincoln set us free?!"

Brothaman: "Says who my Brotha?"

Streetz: "That's what I was taught in school."

Brothaman: "Brotha, when the Europeans enslaved some of us and created a system to keep us enslaved for life, do you actually think a European descendant, Abraham Lincoln, who identified himself as a white man, would seriously consider slaves that Europeans benefited from economically and politically, would set us free?"

"Honest Abe, as he is called, was never about setting our people free that was enslaved. In fact, in his inaugural speech on March 4, 1861, Lincoln said that slavery was legal under the constitution, and had no rights or intention of abolishing slavery. Honest Abe even forced the Fugitive Slave Act in the U.S. constitution."

Streetz: "But Abraham Lincoln created the Civil War to free our people that were slaves in the south, Bruh!"

Brothaman: "No, Brotha. The civil war was started when Abraham Lincoln wrote and made an Emancipation Proclamation."

Streetz: "Emancipation what?!"

Brothaman: "Emancipation means to have ownership or purchaser in Latin. In other words, the North or the Federal government was claiming ownership or saying they purchased the slaves in the south. Abraham Lincoln was a President under the Union or Federal Government of the Northern States. Basically, Abraham Lincoln made the Emancipation Proclamation when it was brought to his attention that the Union for Federal (Northern) Government was losing the civil war to the south."

"The south, the Confederate Government, was beating the Northern Union soldiers badly. Abraham's best general in the Union Army, a man named William T. Sherman, advised Abraham Lincoln it was the Union's best bet to free some of the slaves or make it appear like the slaves were free in order to be recruited and fight for the Union Army."

"The Confederate or Southern Army was already using this tactic promising some slaves that they would be freed, or emancipated, having ownership of self, as well as be allowed to purchase their families if they fought for the Confederacy to keep slaves that didn't fight for the Confederate slaves. Basically, keeping the system in the South alive."

"Therefore Abraham Lincoln wrote and declared an Emancipation Proclamation in 1863 in order to recruit slaves willing to fight for the Union Army. The same tactic is used to recruit some of us in their military today. They promise you freedom, but they still own you or purchase you when they recruit you. Their laws made us slaves forever because slavery was about the economic ownership of property used to enrich the slave owners. Basically, the Civil War was about the North robbing the South for the ownership and free labor the Southern masters amassed. This free labor gave the south unlimited political, as well as an economic power, and the North covet that political and economic power."

Streetz: (appears to be thinking about all Brothaman just said about the purpose for the Civil War)

Streetz: "Man, they don't tell you that stuff in school. All I was taught in school was that Black people were always slaves and Abraham Lincoln set us free in Amerika."

Brothaman: "Were you taught that slavery was about us being Black?"

Streetz: "Yeah. Even in church, I was taught that Black people are cursed people because of the sins of Ham, who's supposed to be the origin of the Black race. Ham, one of Noah's sons, supposedly looked at his father's nakedness and Noah cursed him and his seeds. Ah, man! Now, that I think about it, they are trying to say that a Black man was the first homosexual for looking at his father's nakedness."

Brothaman: "Yep!

Streetz: "That's some bullshit, my nigga!"

Brothaman: "It's a shame when your own people tell us that crap! It's all lies, Bruh. It was a way to make us believe or accept being so-called inferior to the European race. Just like when we were branded and told to accept that degrading philosophy, like how you always said my nigga to your own people."

Streetz: "Man…"

Brothaman: "Brotha look. Enslavement of us was about getting money and using money to get political and military power for the few who could become masters of humanity. It was never about us being the color of Black. In fact, they envied our genetic structure. You can even see that today by how they are willing to get skin cancer by laying under tanning beds or laying out in the sun trying to get some color on their skin. Don't be fooled. Slavery was never about being Black."

Brothaman continues: "The first Europeans that made it over here came weak and uncivilized. Europe was trying to empty their prisons and ethnic cleanse their lands by getting rid of all the undesirables, the worst of the worst; prostitutes and the disease ridden. These undesirables Europe sent away was expected to die, but ended up becoming a potential pilot program for colonization when those undesirables made it to this place now called Amerika."

"At first the British Crown tried to enslave the undesirables they sent away until word got back that they made it. The British Crown saw a potential means of expanding their rule by using the undesirables as slaves, but these European undesirables rebelled in this country what is called the Amerikan Revolution. The British Crown's best and the European undesirables became Amerikans and took over the British colonies."

Brothaman continues: "But, the undesirables who became known as Amerikans weren't righteous and turned arrogant after defeating the British Crown. Still, the undesirables who became Amerikans were able to form an alliance with the British Crown, and together the Amerikans and the British Crown decided on enslaving the Native Americans; the people known as Indians."

Brothaman continues: "Even though the undesirable Europeans would have never survived on this continent without the help from the Indians, the undesirable Europeans, once they got a thirst for power, wanted this continent for themselves and turned on the Indians trying to enslave them. But, the Indians rebelled and refused to be enslaved because all the Indians ever knew was how to be free and one with nature. Yet, in the end, the undesirable Europeans and the British Crown prevailed against the Indians due to better weaponry and deception, by getting the Indian tribes to turn on one another and infecting the Indians with diseases like smallpox, hepatitis, and syphilis."

"Diseases that were native for Europeans, but foreign to the Indians. Yet, they still couldn't force the Indians into slavery, but they almost exterminated the whole Indian race trying to. Being that they couldn't successfully enslave the Indian race, the European undesirables resorted to forming a compromise with the remaining Indians and placed the Indians on Reservations, land that wasn't favorable enough for survival. Nonetheless, the Indians still survived and they were left alone."

Brothaman: "However, it was discovered that Afrikans could labor under extreme conditions and thrive in most environments. Some Africkans were kidnapped or immigrated to Europe and thrived on this continent. Therefore, the Europeans knew Afrikans could adapt in Amerika without falling prey to the elements on this continent. Also, they knew we had the skills to build civilizations… the Greeks, Romans, and the Portuguese, learned this when they came to Afrika to study from us which was recorded in European history."

"The European undesirables who became known as Amerikans, the British Crown, and the Vatican, agreed that the Afrikan race should be enslaved and become slaves to them."

Streetz: "But why didn't we fight them? We just let them put us into slavery?!"

Brothaman: "Nah, our enslavement wasn't that easy and simple. Many fought and won, but they were still able to take a few of us through deception, superior weaponry, or outright kidnapping when they found some Afrikans separated from their tribes."

Streetz: "But I was taught that Afrikans sold Afrikans to the Europeans."

Brothaman: "Yes, some of them did, that's correct. But that wasn't the main reason why 800,000 Afrikans ended up enslaved in the Amerikas and the places known as the Caribbeans."

"The Afrikans that kidnapped and sold Afrikans for the Europeans were either defectors or outcasts of their tribes. Being that Afrikans didn't have prisons like European countries when the tribe captured an enemy, sometimes they were sold or traded to the Europeans, not having a clue what would happen to the enemy once sold."

Brothaman continues: "The Europeans were keen to notice the appearance of different tribes in Afrika. Therefore, they used this to their advantage by spreading discord amongst tribes turning them against each other. They still use this tactic on us to this day here in Amerika, as well as abroad. These tactics are issued through religion and when we became gangs claiming different neighborhoods that we don't own. Or being allowed to appear to accept some of us in their schools, neighborhoods, or businesses. They use our poverty, miseducation, and our desperation as a tool to turn us against one another and tricked us into doing the work for them. It's the business of enslaving and keeping our own people in slavery. Europeans are master manipulators and the only powers they have are deception and the control of illusions."

Streetz: "Well, what I'm getting from you is that slavery was about getting money. So if that's the case all we have to do is get enough money to get free right?"

Brothaman: "No my Brotha. We have to do more than get money to completely be emancipated from them."

Streetz: "But the lack of money is what's keeping us slaves right?"

Brothaman: "Listen Brotha. The first step towards our emancipation is first realizing that we as a people are asleep and have been for four hundred and two years. We need to realize who and what we are. We have to re-educate ourselves and each other. We have to deprogram ourselves and each other from the slave mentalities. We have to become a nation with our own cultural language and politics and have organized collective economical power. As long as we are divided and don't know who we are, we will be owned by them, and our children and grandchildren will be purchased by them. The cycle of our enslavement will continue."

Brothaman continues: "See, our bodies, our physical strength and endurance over the strain of any situation wasn't the only 'natural resource' used to make this country the wealthiest and strongest military power on earth. Our minds were used to. We are naturally creative people due to the rich resources we naturally possess, like soul and melanin. Why do you think they have a pyramid on the back of the dollar bill? We are the first builders of civilization. So when Donald Trump said "Let's make Amerika great again," that was a code to mobilize European descendants to regain control of our minds and use our creative sources to build Amerika back up by using their forefather's system of enslavement. People were starting to come together under the Obama administration. Under the Obama administration, European descendants were trying to be more like us and were moving away from the mentality of us being slaves to them. Everybody wants to be us!"

Streetz: "But I still can't understand how they could keep enslaving us for so long if it is known that we are the first builders of civilizations and that our minds are naturally creative."

Brothaman: "The point is, when you are a slave, your mind doesn't belong to you. For example, we invented a lot of things in this country while being enslaved which the Europeans call 'Intellectual Property'. Yet, being a slave, they weren't allowed to patent and take credit for their inventions. Instead, slave owners took credit for the things we invented. Like Henry Blair, who was a Black inventor in the 1830s who invented the Mechanical Corn Harvester and the Mechanical Seed Planter. But since he was a slave, it allowed his slave owner to get the credit and the money made from it. Hell, they're even trying to make it seem like they created Hip Hop. The way they have been allowed to exploit this culture we created due to us still being dependent on them for our survival. Even though we created Hip Hop, the European descendants make all the money and give the artist crumbs, because the artist gives them complete control over the marketing of their art. The artist has a slave mentally not knowing how valuable their art, creativity, or inventions are. The artist loses the credit and control over their 'Intellectual Property', in other words, their minds."

Streetz: (looking down at the ground, shaking his head)

Brothaman continues: "You see, when they enslaved some of us in order to keep us slaves, they knew they had to erase anything 'Afrikan' from within and around us. Yet, they had to figure out a way to keep us disconnected from our true nature, but connected enough to keep creating for them."

"Our true environment, Afrika, made us extremely powerful as a people. Afrika, being the richest continent on this planet, was a source of infinite energy connected directly to our minds and our bodies. They discovered how easy we could be made to forget our names, our cultures, languages, and even our eating habits. They knew if they could replace our names with their names, cultures (religions), language, and eating habits, we would undoubtedly become their slaves. It was like snatching a lion from its mother and pride when it's a cub and letting it be raised by hyenas. If a lion is raised by hyenas, that lion would grow up thinking he is what?"

Streetz: " A hyena, yo!"

Brothaman: "Exactly! And, that's how they put us, and are still keeping us, in slavery. Like your last name suggests. Whitehead means one who thinks and acts like a European, but not one."

Streetz: "That's phucked up, my nigga."

Brothaman: "Brainwashing and re-programming our minds to be European-like keeps us from remembering ourselves, as well as keeping us divided as a people. Our natures have become no more than a circus. It's like we are tamed, trained, and domesticated animals, used to entertain and feed European ringmasters and butchers."

Streetz: (once again stands silently looking at the ground)

Brothaman: "The key to our manumission relies on the discovery of our 'True History' as a people. We have a Glorious and Shameless past, my Brotha. They know our true history, which they have stored in their museums, libraries, overpriced colleges, and zoos."

"They even go to the jungle of Afrika and learn from the primitive people there. But you must understand that being primitive is not such a bad thing. They make it seem like being primitive is backward, retarded, or docile. It's their way of trying to get us to shun or be afraid of our own people so they can go in and get ancient knowledge from our people in those jungles to use for their self collective enhancement. But understand that primitive means *first* or origin, therefore when they call our people in the jungles primitive, they are really acknowledging our origin and natural sources to be found amongst our own people."

"There, in the jungles of Afrika, amongst the primitive Afrikans, our people still retain ancient knowledge, sciences, and medicines. The Europeans discreetly go seek from our primitive people under the façade of being missionaries. At the same time, these 'missionaries' purpose is to remove the primitive people from their natural habitat, because the Europeans that are in power want it all. They seek to learn how to discover natural resources they could use to control and harness nature's holistic energies. Once they learn from the primitive peoples, they go back to their country and teach our Grand Source of knowledge, sciences, and medicines, to their own people. They hide our knowledge through the use of symbolism, like using animations (cartoons) and movies, to teach their children. The higher knowledge is taught in their high-priced Ivy League colleges, in private ceremonies, in certain fraternity orders, and masonic lodges that we aren't allowed to join."

Streetz: "But, why would we teach the Europeans all this stuff if they have proven to be our enemies. I don't get that shit!"

Brothaman: "First of all, all Europeans aren't our enemies, Bruh. When I speak about the Europeans I am basically talking about their system, their culture, their collective ideologies they use to seek world domination over melanated people worldwide. There have been plenty of Europeans who have rebelled and fought with us to eradicate slavery, like a man named John Brown, who gave his life trying to get weapons for slaves. He lost his life and his sons sacrificed their lives for our cause as well."

"Anyway, if you look at the history of our people, you will see how we are humane people, even when people are doing us wrong. We as a people, traveled before the enslavement of some, and you will never find in our history where we came across others different from us and tried to enslave them. Nor are we the creators of racism. We have never sought world domination as a people. When we came across others different from us, we naturally shared our knowledge, science, and medicines, with them. Hell, we didn't even have prisons in ancient times. When you look at the present state in free Afrika, you don't see or hear about our people trying to enter the nuclear arms race, even though the continent has the resources and the scientific knowledge to build nuclear bombs. Our people naturally know it's not wise to create something that could destroy the whole planet. We aren't about that life!"

Streetz: "But, yo! We continue to teach them things that they use to better themselves and use against us. Now that I think about it, we taught them Hip Hop and they are using the culture to better their lives, but using it to destroy and keep us divided as a people and slaves to them!"

Brothaman: "Now you are starting to see. But you must understand that it's in our nature to want to see all live better. A lot of our people in the past, and the present, who teach or introduce them to a better way of life, didn't know that the knowledge and wisdom would be used to destroy. European's by nature are individualistic people, while we are collectivist people. Most melonated people are collectivist by nature, meaning we are family-oriented, while European's are singular-minded people. They don't like to share. That's why it's a class society in their system and why they believe in the mentality of the 'have and have nots'."

Streetz: "But doesn't knowledge suppose to make you better? It seems like the more knowledge they get, the more they divide, conquer, and destroy."

Brothaman: "Knowledge without wisdom makes knowledge a destructive tool. For example, their history shows how knowledge without the understanding of it made them envious, greedy, and selfish. At their conquest, once they got the knowledge, but didn't understand the knowledge they received, they went back and destroyed the civilizations they learned from. They raided our libraries and murdered elders, the scribes who were the retainers of our way of life. They stole our artifacts, raided graves, hidden treasures, and destroyed the knowledge they couldn't understand. After hijacking and destroying civilizations they could conquer, they went back to their lands rearranged our history, and plagiarized the knowledge they could understand."

Streetz: "Plagiarizing?"

Brothaman: "Meaning they stole our knowledge and made it appear like they were the originators or the source of something. But, the knowledge they plagiarized from us made them destructive. For one, our understanding of knowledge gave our people the wisdom to see how everyone and everything in creation is connected. And when this oneness is disconnected, everyone and everything becomes unbalanced and destructive."

All melanized people on the planet universally understood this. Some knowledge wasn't meant for them, because naturally they can't understand oneness, a spiritual principle, not a mental one. That's why you see how every place they have traveled to has been like Metastatic Cancer aggressively attacking the system of nature. They destroy and capture animals for their consumption, or entertainment. They destroy land out of greed and selfishness, and seek to conquer natural inhabitants of the lands they come across out of envy, greed, and want to exploit for themselves. Knowledge without wisdom, also made them arrogant and self-entitled. They don't believe in 'we'. Their systems are built around the idea of 'me' and 'mine'. The Europeans in power know that true history is the seat of power and a glitch to their system of bondage or slavery."

Streetz: "Well, shit my nigga. If they done stole our knowledge and destroyed most of it, then we will never know who we are."

Brothaman: "The knowledge they could understand has been preserved, which they keep stored in their libraries, their museums, in Greek mythology, the Bible, and even in their zoos."

Streetz: "Zoo's?!"

Brothaman: "Yes, in their zoos too. You see the study of Zoology is their way of learning about nature in a simplified form. Our concept of nature is oneness."

Streetz: "Man zoology sounds like the study of animals. So you sayin' we can learn about ourselves from studying animals?"

Brothaman: "Yeah, you can. In nature, our bodies, or our flesh, is similar to animals. Basically, our bodies are created from the same elements and minerals that make up an animal's body. Remember, our concept of nature is oneness. Everyone and everything in nature is connected. Everyone and everything physically, are connected because everyone and everything physically contains the elements and minerals of nature. So, learning about animal anatomy shows them how to understand the physical aspects of the human body in nature's creation. But, they use this knowledge of zoology to tame, control, and exploit, the physical and biological aspects of nature for power and material wealth. They don't just capture animals to be put in zoos for entertainment or to preserve so-called endangered species. In fact, certain animals only become endangered when they come across them. Melanated people didn't have any zoos, or just killed animals for sport. However, when melanated people killed animals, it was either to protect themselves or out of a need to survive. Our people could study animals in the wild and learn about the nature of our bodies without capturing animals or purposely killing them. You can learn more about animals that are wild in their natural habitats while they are alive, rather than dead, or in an unnatural environment like simulated environments called zoos."

Streetz: "Brothaman, you know all that shit sounds crazy right?!"

Brothaman ignores the comment and continues: "Not only is the knowledge of us preserved in their institutions like their zoos, schools, museums, Greek Mythology, and their Bibles. The knowledge of us is preserved in the jungles of Africka."

Streetz: (cuts Brothaman off) "Man, I ain't goin' ta no jungle!"

Brothaman: "You don't have to. The knowledge of us can be found in the urban cities from those who have knowledge of self, in our art, our musicals, and our dances. But more importantly, the knowledge of self can be found by activating our souls and melanin. Knowledge of self can be found in our subconscious mind, the seat of our memory base. Who we are is reserved and preserved right there in our memory, something they couldn't capture or enslave. Why, because as long as nature lives, our souls and melanin will naturally absorb and record nature. No matter where we are or where we are born, we will always be surrounded by nature, because everyone and everything created comes from nature. We can even learn the knowledge about us and the wisdom of our true nature in their Bible."

Streetz: "Man, the Bible full of contradiction. I don't care about no Bible, Bruh!"

Brothaman: "That's only because you don't know how to read the Bible. You see they were able to hide our history in the Bible because they know we couldn't understand the English and Latin languages. They also count on us being disconnected from nature and not knowing about symbology. Like why are Ethiopia and Egypt mentioned in the Bible more than any other nations? In fact, when you think of Ethiopia and Egypt, if you look these two words up, you will see that Ethiopia and Egypt derive from the Greek (European) language. So, you would think that the Bible is talking about great people from Greece. But if you know that they are talking about 'us' as a people in Afrika, then you will clearly understand the symbology, and how they use symbology languages and false images to fool and enslave our minds. Ethiopia is called Abyssinia and Egypt is called Kemet by our people in ancient Afrika."

Streetz: "I never heard of Abyssinia or Kemet."

Brothaman: "Well, Abyssinia is the place called the cradle of civilization where all life originated and descended from. And Kemit created the greatest universities known to man. They were elite universities that we created called the Pyramids."

Streetz: "But, I was taught that the Pyramids are tombs where we buried the dead."

Brothaman: "Nah, the pyramids were elite universities in ancient times in Afrika! The Pyramids were for the living, not the dead. People went to the Pyramids to find and activate life, not to learn and practice necromancy."

Streetz: "Necromancy?!"

Brothaman: "Necromancy means communication with the dead."

Streetz: "But now that I think about it, wasn't there a book found long ago in the pyramids called 'The Book of the Dead'?"

Brothaman: "Bruh, the book was in fact called 'The Book of Coming Forth by Day' by our people. When they raided the pyramids they found this book buried in some of the Pharoah's sarcophagus and couldn't interpret the language we wrote it in and thought it was a book containing the practice of necromancy. Like I mentioned earlier, some knowledge isn't meant for them. He called this book the Coming Forth By Day because the Day represents Light, and Light represents life. We as a people, don't believe in death. We know that light is infinite energy and energy is a continuous flow of life. Therefore, no one or anything animated with life ever dies, it only changes forms. Like when an animal appears to die like a human being. If the body's buried naturally in the ground, the body becomes one with the earth and actually fertilizes the earth. And what happens when something fertilizes the earth?"

Streetz: "Things grow from the earth!"

Brothaman: "Right! So you see…life continues. There is no such thing as death or the final thing of life. However, in their cultures when something appears to be without energy they believe it's dead, that it doesn't have any more energy."

Brothaman: "Another example I would like to point out is how they try to hide the knowledge of us in the Bible through symbology. When you read the Bible and come across anything where they are talking about lions, you will know they are talking about us, because lions come from where?"

Streetz: "Afrika!"

Brothman: "Absolutely, Bruh!"

Streetz: "I hear you my nigga. But to keep it real, I'm just trying to live from day to day. Ain't got no time to be worried about no history. The past is the past my nigga. Our history ain't goin' to put no food on my table yo!"

Brothaman: (sighs) "Is sitting in prison playing cards, watching T.V., playing dominos, talking about what you use to do in the streets, the drugs you sold, the brotha's you robbed, the cars you had, all the weed you smoked, or the girls you had sex with, putting food on your table?!"

Streetz: "Man, it's all about getting money, my nigga! Without money, a nigga can't live, yo!"

Brothaman: "Yet, in prison, as well as out there, you can't support yourself because you haven't figured out how to get real money."

Streetz: "I eat every night my nigga!"

Brothaman: "What, cakes, chips, and twenty-five-cent soups?! That shit harms your mind and body and at the same time provides revenue that helps fund the prison industry, keeping guys like you and me incarcerated. It helps to keep your people out there financially impoverished when they send you money, which could be used to start a business of some kind. All it does is add more stress to your people out there who are struggling themselves trying to look out for you in here, especially with the Covid-19 pandemic putting people out of work. But do you care, though?!"

Streetz: (smiles) "That's the way it is my nigga."

Brothaman: (shaking his head) "Pure selfishness, my Brotha. That attitude will never take you far in life."

Streetz: "Look my nigga. When I was out there making that paper, my people didn't care where I got it from as long as I got it and gave them some of it. It's only right they look out for me now. Yo' problems go away when you got plenty of paper and everybody respects you my nigga!"

Brothaman: "People don't respect you because you have money. They covet and only tolerate you long enough to get money or material things from you, all the while they are plotting on how to take your place and remove you from the picture. There is no honor or respect in negativity, taking penitentiary chances, or risking your life trying to accumulate those dead presidents by selling drugs or robbing your people. You think your problems will go away? Man, that proves you are fresh in the game and more confused than you try to make yourself otherwise not seem."

"Drug money is blood money. Families and communities are destroyed because of it. Drug money brings hate, envy, greed, jealousy, and debauchery, making you vulnerable and prey to diseases and unnecessary deaths."

Streetz: "Thought you said there's no such thing as death?!"

Brothaman: "Man, listen! If you think your problems end once you acquire money from drug sales and robberies, you are sadly mistaken. You're just setting up for steady failure bringing unnecessary hardships to you, your family, and your community. Money, even legally, won't take all your problems away. In fact, in a capitalist society, it'll bring more problems. You can never get enough paper money to solve all your problems. Paper money is only promissory notes, creating the illusion that you are obtaining wealth, which you have to keep selling your labor to maintain basic essentials in capitalist society if you don't have the machinery and codes to print those federal reserve bills. Plus, if you are a consumer using the paper money to buy a bunch of nonsense, you'll still remain poor living like a desperate wild beast when it can no longer find food or get enough money."

"The paper money is not what makes the wealthy, wealthy, but it can be used to help you climb up the steps to wealth. If used cunningly, paper money can be used as a medium for exchange to get to real wealth. Paper money is a source of grading on the lower economic scale or system, for those who have no real wealth. What makes a poor person rise to the world of the wealthy is not by how much money you accumulate. It's about how you can creatively use it once you accumulate enough of it and use those promissory notes to purchase real wealth. Paper money ain't nothing unless it has some real value (wealth) backing it."

Streetz: "What's the real wealth my nigga?!"

Brothaman: "What backs those dollar bills and makes them valuable is the control monopoly and exploitation of the land. All kinds of land have carried some kind of resource that could be used to create wealth, meaning the unlimited stream of energy being used. Money is nothing more than saying energy. Money is energy and you become wealthy when you can control and exploit energy."

"If you want to see how valuable those dead presidents are alone, just take $5,000 or $10,000 to a bank and try to get a loan to start a business, purchase a home, or even a car, and see what they'll ask you. They are going to ask you what kind of collateral do you have that could be put up. Bankers care less about how much paper money you have when you seek a loan. They can't sell paper money if you can't pay back the loan. Paper money is only for poor and middle-class people to use for consumption purposes and to pay off debts."

Streetz: "But, isn't paper money energy too?"

Brothaman: "Yeah, but it only has a temporary stimulant feel. It can never stand as an unlimited stream of energy source by itself. Think about it. If you lose paper money or if you burn it up, it's gone."

Streetz: "Man just look at Oprah, Bill Cosby, Bob Johnson, or even Michael Jordan. Them niggas are billionaires and they are wealthy my nigga!"

Brothaman: "But what do they own besides Oprah that white folks don't control? Oprah is the only one that can be considered wealthy. Oprah owns and controls her own T.V. Network. Oprah can hire and pay Black Folks on her own and make decisions without seeking approval from white folks because of her ownership. Oprah is emancipated and is an example of being her owner. This is what makes you wealthy."

Streetz: (cut Brothaman off) "But Bob Johnson had his own T.V. Network...B.E.T., right?"

Brothaman: "Had, yeah. But he still had to go through white folks in order to get it distributed on cable networks.

And then look who he sold Black Entertainment Television too… Viacom. A entainment company owned by a European decedent company. Once sold to Viacom, look at how they took off all the major news and inspirational programs and replaced B.E.T contents with mostly ratched entertainment. It's Black Entertainment Television, but owned by white folks. It's a joke, Bruh!"

Streetz: "Shit, I don't blame Bob Johnson. That nigga became a billionaire because he sold B.E.T. I would have sold my company too for that kind of doe!" (laughs)

Brothaman: "Selling B.E.T. only made him rich, not wealthy."

Streetz: "Phuck ya talkin' 'bout. Being rich means being wealthy, my nigga!"

Brothaman: "It's not the same. The rich and the wealthy aren't the same, they're not equal. Just like the middle class are rich, but aren't considered wealthy compared to the upper class. The wealthy are in positions of power and own and control Natural and Human Resources. The wealthy own countries, governments, militaries, politics, and dictates how energy, whether limited or unlimited, will be used. The wealthy create the economy and decide how the wealth will be distributed. The wealthy do not, and will not, sell their 'Intellectual Property'. They instead use it to control and exploit those who don't own land or control energy. So tell me where does Bob Johnson, Michael Jordan, or Bill Cosby have that kind of power? They are billionaires, right? Look, how they put a Billionaire in prison (Bills Cosby), for so-called raping white women thirty years ago!"

"Yeah, Bob Johnson, Michael Jordan, and Bill Cosby are billionaires, but they have the kind of money that can be taken from them if the wealthy decides it should be taken. Hell, look at Jordan. He has been a slave to Nike for years. The rich only have temporary power. Temporary economic stimulated power is like caffeine…it stimulates for a while, but it doesn't last. That's the kind of money power Bob Johnson, Michael Jordan, and Bills Cosby have."

Streetz: "Man you trippin my nigga! You can't be from the hood. Niggas in the hood don't talk like you do and you sound like a hater."

Brothaman: "Bruh, I am from the hood and I'm as hood as it gets, that's why I have been in prison all these years. I just choose not to be stuck in a nigga mentality anymore. I hurt my people out there for what?! Too many of our people died trying to help our people, to keep us from being in the situation you and I are in right now. And I'm supposed to keep acting like a nigga?! I woke up Brotha! I'm not about being stuck, confined for the rest of my life to a system that seeks to keep people in the hood or in prison."

Streetz: "Man niggas..." (Brothaman interrupts Streetz because he's tired of hearing that word nigga.)

Brothaman: "Look, why would I want to be a nigga?! Being a nigga means being the worst of the worst. Niggas don't think for themselves, nor act or talk rationally. Niggas always make the wrong choices because they don't understand how to make the right choices. Where is niggaland? Where are the nigga governments, their schools, military structures, their political and collective economic power? Are niggas represented at the United Nations? Is there a flag representing the Niggas?!"

Streetz: (Staring off looking perplexed)

Brothaman continues: "Niggas aren't a force other nations respect. In fact, niggas don't even respect other niggas. Nigga is a state of mind, a fabricated idea used to belittle and degrade a whole nation of people, US! That word nigga is derived from the word nigger. I overstand that some of our people thought they could take ownership of this word and take power from the racist denigration of the word by changing this word nigger to nigga. Still, the word nigga couldn't be shifted to have a more positive connotation and image. The word nigga still doesn't empower us. When you mention the word nigga you can still feel the degradation of it and you definitely conjure up a negative picture when you say and hear the sound of nigga. Psychologically, when you hear nigga, you automatically think the worst of a person, prejudging them to be negative. We have to change the whole concept and the sound of the word nigga if we want to empower ourselves and our people."

"That's why I call you Brotha instead of nigga. I see your true nature or essence which is good, not that degraded image you were tricked into thinking you are. Nigga is a word, an idea, and sound, designed to express hatred of self, and those who look like you which has perpetuated Brothas, destroying Brothas. Brotha's destroying our women, our women destroying our children, where the children become a reflection of the nigga mentality growing up destroying themselves, others, and our communities, which is already dilapidated due to the nigga syndrome. Even N.W.A. tried to tell us that nigga is an attitude of destruction."

Streetz: "It's just slang, yo!"

Brothaman: (Throws his hands up) "You just don't get it do you?!"

Streetz: "Get what?!"

Brothaman: "That word nigga has power over our minds and helps create negative conditions in our lives. Or how words, especially how names, have the power to decide how we are perceived by self and others, creates images of you, whether negative or positive. Words are thoughts, and the wrong word, names, or thoughts, can control, manipulate, and exploit, us whether by us or by others?! Look around this prison yard. The majority of the people in prison are us because we thought and acted like niggas!"

An announcement is made over the PA system.

"The yard is now closed for Gray Unit. All inmates report to their assigned dorms and prepare for chow!"

Streetz: "Shit is crazy man!"

Brothaman: (smiles) "I know my Brotha. I know. But it doesn't have to be once you realize 'What Time It Really Is!'"

As Streetz walks away someone calls out to him: "Yo, Toby, what up my nigga?!"

Streetz looks at Brothaman, and Brothaman shakes his head, then headed to his prison cell.

To be continued…

Part Two

The Wailing Prisoner:

Conscious Cries of
a Smiling Prisoner

Attention

Experiences are limited when you
live in a gothic environment

Lost personalities turn to mimic

Copying what they see on T.Vs and hearing on radios

Suspended minds doing time behind time…

Conquered by seconds, minutes, and hours

Replicas trapped in forgetfulness devolving into mannequins

Early stages of their lives treated like equines

The "Projects" are bidding grounds for
kapitalistic real-estate equestrians

Public schools adding to the drowsiness

Real lessons are disseminated like
Salem witches burned to ashes

Unable to communicate mouths deflates becoming beaks

No more rhythm when they speak,

The language and sound of origin was
taken by the Afrikan Holocaust

This means minds became cataract eyes
on the inside dim and bleak

Bajah Oginga Langley

Still experiencing the curse or Will Lynch when they sleep

Shape-shifting when they are awake inhaling mold and lead

Raised off kool-aid and processed bread addicted to sugar

Historical events and accomplishments
deleted from the subconscious

Systemic racism rearranged the conscious
to reflect self-hate

Then given jobs that would display a parade of foolishness

Flatline minds turn to crime to survive too young to copulate

But do it anyway, leaving babies to feed wolves and eagles

When they get arrested or die young

Even human vultures get a plate and a seat at the table

While Soul Rebels on their soapboxes
advocating Black Power resuscitation

But unable to connect…the majority
rather thrive off of amnesia.

Programmed to disregard their own quintessence

Remaining weak and easily manipulated

Accepting without questioning the nigger branding

Infected with illusive symbols of power…
sex, cocaine, heroin, codeine,

K-2 temporary self-esteem, tight jeans,
rainbow banes and artificial manes

The Prison Philosopher

Cartoon dreaming…written, directed
and produced by gothic Europeans

Facts!

Or some become ex-brutes able to hide
under tailored suits and ties

Never to coeternity with their own kind…

Happy to be accepted, briefly, in corporate Amerikkka

Bajah Oginga Langley

Experimental Projects

The Projects is just that…A Project!

It's designed to manufacture and experiment
on infantiled animalism

Either way, the Projects was created to intercept lost souls

Those born without guidance in the womb.

Projects are a project constructed to turn light into shadows
by pseudoscientists, racist biologists, and mutated
archaeologists given jobs to turn souls in holograms big
corporations own and puppeteer

Until lost souls become skulls and bones

Once enough energy is extracted and
assimilated into their DNA.

In the Projects Lost souls are kept infinite sleep

Imagine Ancient People captured to be Fossil fuels

Used to fuel the artificial rejects stuck in sound effects

Attacking your true cause for existing

If you don't learn your true purpose and meaning

You stay stuck in a district fueling and
refueling the project conductors

Going from project to prison

No more than a recycled Project in a prison.

What If

If I ascended to the sky, then descended…

Would you catch me?

If I was rich, but then you come to my home
and realize I was poor…

Would you still yearn for me?

If I told you my soul was older than this world…

Would you laugh and banish me?

If I was a Spark speaking to you in the dark…

Would you fan me?

If you knew I am the Tree, and you are the Life…

Would we be priceless, or would you sell us to society?

Bajah Oginga Langley

AI vs the Human Psyche

Madness…Millions are addicted to viral nonsense

Common sense is devalued in the 21st century because computation threw a south par and struck the minds of the gullible… thanks to the creators of Windows

The shocking revelation?

Intelligent reasoning is becoming more irrelevant now that artificial intelligence, a matrix, was given power to control the souls of Human thinking and production

Effectively AI does the calculations and
the gullible end up dead batteries.

Pokemon go or castle building chasing illusionary entities

An easy distraction creating mental discombobulation,

Extracting Human energy to give life
to computerized deities

Crypto currencies like Bitcoin is the new God in we trust

Gotta move instantly in a 'cloud' in a society inflated with computation industrialization, but the trade-off?

You age quickly like a canine blinded to reality

Enthralled by the web of electronic algorithms
where Spam is I AM

Junk mail invading the medulla oblongata private spaces

The Prison Philosopher

Minds online caught by the Net that steals the
Works of the brain's chemical impulses
Stimulated by the artificial pace.

Taken over by smartphones and tablets

Touch screens and voice audio turn into
An induced euphoria, thought suspended in a
Dimension of web animation.com

Lost in a virtual that's not reality…

Hey, where did the minds go?!

Bajah Oginga Langley

Thieves

Watch out for the thieving eyes

Those predator eyes watching you as you come up

The dark yellow eyes howling inside searching for prey

Human animals that haven't evolved yet.

In the world of the materialistic…Love is despised

Hate and Envy are the kings and queens here

The inevitable flaming wicks are too bright
Hate and envy excoriate here

This world use to be inhabited by Third -eyes

But, too much abomination rose up

Ascended then blended in with the Incorporeal

Some Incorpeareals fell in love with sensations

And, gave birth to material mutations

The degenerated was watered and given sunshine

Declined was the Incorporeal that fell victim to the
dirty aspects of mutated kleptomania

In time mutated kleptomaniacs rose to be the new scientists

The outnumbered Incorpeals had to escape from this planet

The Prison Philosopher

Too many had died in this kleptomaniac war

Incorporeal weakened couldn't survive
the Kleptomania mutiny

Thieving eyes took over with materialism

Bajah Oginga Langley

The Convicted

Reflecting on the different ways the gates of hell
prevails within the minds of the convicted

No cloak for the ignorance of many incarcerated
submerged in insane habitats

The omen prediction, projected violence to come, when
ignorance dances to the tune of collective exasperation

Creating a whole new regiment swarming like wild locusts

While a high percentage of loyal
religionist send prayers to oblivion

Hoping to resuscitate a new Moses intoxicated
and prostrated by religion

The Counter Intelligence Program (COINTEL Pro) continues to
search for the chosen out to execute the First Borns

Melanin under the microscope and soul in a choke hold
by the system of acculturation

Damn!

Life was designed to be an evolutionary experience, a
continuous movement for transcendental transactions

But the interconnection had been cut, separated, and isolated

Producing foster children in the earth's ecosystem

This is how the criminal subculture became the replacement
breeding learning disabilities with no therapeutic solution

The Prison Philosopher

Unless you are from the privileged class,
the one-dimensional generations using economic privilege as a
pass to justify condescending the underclass

Broken with a faded identity

You aren't seen as human

Hands up, don't shoot!

Pow!

Black Lives don't matter until…

There's a Black funereal and a chant that says,
"I can't breathe!"

Bajah Oginga Langley

No!

Sitting on a hardened aluminum bench in a cold cell…
they got me!

Staring at the wall mad as hell

Two glopping guards trying to look hard
about to strip search me!

Stand up they say.. remove your shirt,
pants, socks and boxers

Bend over, spread your butt cheeks,
lift up your nut sack and cough

Like this is some kind of strip show

Nah, Phuck that. They ain't effeminating me in this process

Fist clenched tight ready to swing on this process

Refusing to be molested by a system that demoralizes nature

However, sadist surrounds me ready to pounce on me

Refusing to cooperate, which means
refusing to break up on arrival!

Non-Violence vs Violence… Who's Stronger?

Humility… They started out marching using Non-Violence
to protest for Freedom, but in a split second, Non-Violence
is runnin', screamin', and duckin' tear gas

Non-Violence is inhaling

At Humility and Non-Violence batons are swingin'

(High Pitched Screamin')

Old Folks on their knees prayin'

National Guards sadistically attackin'

A great sacrifice of blood is spilling for Freedom

Police sirens blarin' and wailin'

Indifference and xenophobia echoes hate on bullhorns shoutin'
"Non-Violence, you ain't American!"

Rocks thrown at defenseless women

Mace sprayed on collegiate students

(High Pitched Screamin')

Non-Violence taking a helluva beatin' for Justice.

Paramedics standing around in confusion

Bajah Oginga Langley

Morticians anticipate the increased value in their occupation

Pressure from a water hose…
down the street Non-Violence goes slidin'

Humility is taking a helluva whippin' for protestin'

Spittle sticks to faces and clothin'

Non-Violence still runnin', screamin', and duckin'

Today, a Peaceful protest undergoes
an execution for Equality

Arrested, Non-Violence is piling up in a Paddy Wagon

Humility branded a felon means…

The law of Jim Crow resurfaces segregation
in the form of mass incarceration

(High Pitched Screamin')

Non-Violence denied the right to vote for
not being opulent and violent enough

Racism and Fascism are allowed free reign by politicians

The media get incentives to record the
Civil Right crucifixions

(The Screaming, The Runnings, The Incarcerations)

No sympathy from the United States presidential corporation

Each administration's mediations "Give poor people Freedom,
Justice and Equality, eh…Out of the bloody question?!

Humility is down

The Prison Philosopher

Non-Violence still runnin' with hands up
pleading for compassion

Cryin' out for help because turning the
other cheek isn't workin'

This is Humility and Non-Violence…

Still, rubber bullets assault their abdomens

A frenzy of violence feasting on Humility and
Non-Violence today is the strongest weapon

Non-Violence who thought peaceful protesting
would be so anti-human and violent?!

Passively, Humility and Non-Violence started out confident and
standin' out ended up runnin', screamin', crawlin'
and incarcerated for humbly thinking…

No one would be so cruel to Non-Violence
the Peaceful Movement right?!

The opportunity for all to be more humane, right?!

Bajah Oginga Langley

The Imperceptible Ordeal

Twelve!

That's the sound of the 5-0, the beast is creeping up

To fill up 1,000 man prisons, even locking women up

Or its confinement under house arrest
or probation supervision

No rehabilitation, only humiliation, and languorousness
because the poor don't know how to
Campaign in the pursuit of happiness

Yet, looking for a way out hoping some divine appeal goes
through, but nothing divine happens

Therefore, many resort to escaping the truth
through debasing methods like licentiousness or
engrossed in decomposing hallucinations.

Addictions makes money seem plentiful in the projects

Until you get arrested due to a slow social development

Now jails are draining funds from all
the blood money accumulated and guns confiscated

You're given an orange jumpsuit and shower shoes,
a sign that you now belong to the state

Drugs in the 'projects' had us thinking we could make it and
escape public housing living in the cheapest way,
where bail bondsmen, lawyers, district attorneys, judges
and some preachers, prey on our illiteracy

The Prison Philosopher

Morticians too, cause Black people in the
projects die at a faster rate

The projects are big businesses for the
municipality in your city

Children growing up lost, abandon, and curious,
roaming the streets like dingos

In the projects our clubs gives us the chance to sweat the pain
off - high all night but waking up in shrouds

Self-hatred runs rampart turning days
and nights into deserts

Thoughts of lust capture the innocent who end up cursed

Preachers preaching sermons for the
worst on pagan's day…

As long as you give 'em money they'll be your nurse

Then they send you back to your projects

All the while the government gathers more data,
organizing the information to do away with all those
performing desolated experiences-

After they make a quick buck!

Bajah Oginga Langley

In Time

Shadow walking

Whistling in a tune with the riddim of nature

Bright showers from the sun bathing my skin

Warriors beating on drums vibratory speaking

The Clouds ready to cry

The Earth bracing for the tears

The Lion's roar giving thanks for another day of pride

Mama's in the kitchen preparing the Healing Oil

Papa in the living room debating politricks
with Uncles and Friends

The Elders predicting…

We soon will be coming in from the cold

Paid to Watch

Private Eyes are paid to pry and spy on the Quicken Eye

Fired by bloodshot corporations infected with Kapitalism
trying to collect Human Treasures

It doesn't make much of a difference if you are a citizen or
some denizen, national, local, commercial or global…

Private Eyes are paid to find Human Minerals concentrated in
environments scattered here and there where Human Treasures
can be found raw, fragmented naïve, and not appraised by self.

The story goes…When Human Jewels were found by Private
Eyes and unwittingly sold to swine by naïve Human Treasures

Human Jewels became National Treasures for
other nations pleasures

Naïve Treasures made the Finders Keepers a Unified Banks

Private Eyes became missionaries for the Unified Banks who
paid Private Eyes to set up Shark Tanks urging Naïve Treasures
to beg the Finders keepers to invest in their worth.

The Finders Keepers incorporated and declared a mission
statement. "If Naïve Treasures don't know how to Appraise,
Market and Manage their true worth…Then, the Unified Banks will
appraise, monopolize, manage and market you for you…
But make naive Treasures pay a poverty fee to appraise,
manage and create a market to market you for you!"

What this amounts to is…

Bajah Oginga Langley

Naïve Human Treasures becomes debts

Where they are no more than Human Credits Cards being
charged for things they can't afford

Because, materially and economically, the Finders Keepers
discovered the naïve appraisals and the fact that naïve Human
Treasures don't know how to appraise themselves, nor know
how to manage and market their true worth themselves.

However, when you discover your Treasure and begin to
appraise yourself and discover that footprint on your
Original Birth Certificate is your life's mortgage
converted into a Trust Fund Deed…

Private Eyes are mobilized to ask you to produce the
Provenance and Providence documents…

The ones that carry the authentic seal of a bonafide Sovereign

This is why Private eyes are paid to pry, spy and
capture the Quicken Eye

The Pyramids don't lie about where and who the Lost
Treasures are excavated and collected from

Streetz of Melancholy

The architecture of the Streetz is designed to be sacrilegious
and socio-economical exploitative to the poor due to poor
depended thinking while prosperous for the penological thinker a
means to attract the poor's Jewel of Ascension

Think impoverishly and make a false
move in the Kapitalist game…

One strike and you can be hauled off to a solar eclipsed
camp warping the penny-ante thinker into a
dimension of sharecropping dementia

Before then…in the streetz, you try to survive and thrive
with a plan to get by foraging for money

Lured by the box Pandora in a country, where broke thinking
turns your business scheme into a penurious hustle in the end

Not knowing how to think to win nor knowing
the rules of investment

How every penny counts, but not if it's consumed up in vanity

So you're inspired by material desires
aroused by animal instincts now

The body floods the mind with animal instincts now

Which is the declination into the animal kingdom now,
while the penological thinker extracts your mineral from
your mental celestial sphere field now

Bajah Oginga Langley

Recruiting and subliminally enticing you
to keep being uncivilized now

Where the eyes will only see and experience
the animal thirst vividly

Clearly trained to be a human sideshow who is
bait for penological investors

Nevertheless, the goal is to get by in the streetz of melancholy

In the streetz of melancholy…it's get high, have unlimited sex,
get doe, have fun, die fast and young, right?

In the streetz not caring about blue skies submissive to the
beneficiaries of fabrication, nor hear love whispering "I Love You"
through the air cloud of trash everywhere raised to don't care

In the streetz lost in a frenzy of a messy,
small portion of consumer feasting those dead presidents
resurrected from poor thinking

More each day, lost growing up to contend in the
greedy consumer's nightmare

The critical attitude of the poor

Some on their knees trying to do right telling the wrong God
this life ain't fair while the rich are living in pomp and grandeur

Won't the poor get caught up lusting for dirty wealth
requiring blood to be sacrificed

Instead of Love thy neighborhood…it's thought success
comes from covet thy neighbor, until they can't breathe
no more submitting to handcuffs as a cure

Too much pressure in the streetz searching
for relief where melancholy reeks

The Prison Philosopher

Taking plea bargains, finding respite in jails and prisons now

Resorting to telling war stories of unschooled
battles glad to live in and for the moment

Then reality sets in and becomes a cheap coffin with your body
laced with make up on and your mouth stitched up

This means the poverty has conquered when the
choir sings slow songs about you, employed for the sole
purpose, knowing one day the unprofitable song would be
reserved for you and others like you…

Who never stop to listen to life and comprehend the official
currency of life's existence.

Bajah Oginga Langley

The Uniform of Oblivion

Arrested…Next stop, Prison!

After being fingerprinted and digitally photographed

You become no more than a number dressed up in irrelevancy

Taken out of existence for a period of time

Where socially and economically, isolated by time

No sociopathic escapes from the dismal penal emporiums-

The projections of dormancy

With enough human power, this abnormal environment gave
birth to a new religion constructed by a few penological sadists

Convicted and sentenced to incarceration concentration…

Gray skies descend upon your head daily

As soon as you put on the uniform of the irrelevant

Your eyes become a coffin forced to close in order to
give a few crypt keepers some oxygen

You grow older from the stress and depression

Your skin becomes paler from lack of vitamin C

Your breathing becomes forgetful each day, you wake
up from being glued to the uniform of stigma

Because you were subtracted from life's balance of color

The Prison Philosopher

You are expected to submit to rules, policies, and procedures…

Those regulated guidelines blueprints form funereal parlors

Your life grows soporific trapped in a phantasm

And, you can't even holla, because if they hear
you that means that you are awake…

Then they will come to restrain and hauled you off

Put into a psychosomatic cell, a paranormal
field used to haunt you

Destroying any residue of rationalization is the Purpose

So they can keep parading you around
in a uniform designed to garnish

The food that causes a natural produce
that fights psychosis and trauma

Man it's hard to think when all you see
and inhale is asbestos paint

Everywhere boxing you in while having to wear a
uniform that mentally and subjectively reeks

No matter how clean you try to keep your mind…

The nightmare continues,

As incarceration keeps you advertised on the prison's menu

Bajah Oginga Langley

The Sound of Ignorance

The targeted underclass don't want to hear that
knowledge shit they love hearing dreams of ignorant shit
dying for engrossing opportune bullshit

Glad to be labeled as misfits of the Amerikan society
skinny boy jeans, tight shirts, blonde wigs, or weave
extended with dead Asian hair and shit

Malt liquor, prepackaged marijuana, concentrated
vaporizers are the new induced high and shit

Sweaty clubs producing delirium impregnated for
government checks not caring about politics

Neighborhoods piled up in psychological feces, but the targeted
underclass don't want to hear that knowledge shit!

Debasing drug sells, drug addictions, senseless intoxications

Idol worshipping despoiled cotton paper dead presidents and
minds rolled up and spiked with psychosomatic delusions

Sleeping briefly paralyzes the body's natural rejuvenation

Stigmatized, and traumatized in nonsense…

Thrust into a realm of the vampire

But the targeted underclass don't want
to hear that knowledge shit!

Well, due to the ignoramous governors, senators, mayors,
city counselors, lawyers, district attorneys, police
departments, judges, politicians and some preachers,

The Prison Philosopher

plus penal institutions receive secured profits

But the targeted underclass don't want
to hear that knowledge shit!

Putrefying fish, chicken, and pork are fried in Project kitchens
the grease is thrown out the windows dilapidating the environment

Children run outside facing the inhalation of death

Meanwhile…

The city buses pick up grandmas and take 'em
to work to be the "Help"

Drunkards standing across the street chanting
"Man, you gotta dime for some wine!"

Shynecka only trying to buy some bread for her mother

But the gangs heckling her purity only see her as a whore

"Man, you gotta dime for some wine!"

Phuck! Someone for sport busted a shot through a car window

Amped up from peer pressure after leaving the Waffle House

Damn! A shot to the heart, she died instantly
crashing into a telephone pole

But the targeted underclass don't want
to hear that knowledge shit!

Across town, a 13-year-old was shot in her right
eye for refusing to be sexually active.

"Man, you gotta dime for some wine!"

Bajah Oginga Langley

Technology creates Facebook crooks sending "Molly" to
the hoods to deface ignorant minds farther down the
rabbit cesspool…the mental comatose road

Every ten years, a census poll is conducted to project how
many more ignorant folks to send down the hole

Why? Because ignorance has been found to be a
liability to nature, law punishing the ones refusing knowledge
sliding down the path of ignorance

Hey boy… Hey gal, it's your fault you are ignorant,
the civil law says, but you like calling yourselves
a nigga and bitches and shit, right?!

Ghetto Victims

You're right!

The ghetto youths are out of control

But blame it on Amerika's promotion of
profanity and debauchery

Ghetto youths are only coping the
stereo-typing and indoctrination

Once desensitized, no more innocence make 'em
strangers to fears lacking empathy

Caught up spiraling downward in an insensible
subculture Amerika created

Born unprotected fighting stages vulnerable to western rages

Growing up in Project cages

Socialized to expect to be incarcerated or die at young ages

Live fast and forget about tomorrow

Though the present has no future for them

Spending their short lives in a mental
cubicle fed unedible education

Most of their school time is spent hearing or
attending their peer's funerals

Bajah Oginga Langley

This is real life in the ghettos nothing subliminal

Try to help 'em and get posted on the F.B.I. wanted list

Remember Fred Hampton tried to do this and
got murdered by a Judas and a black agent

Yet, Black Fists keeps emerging…they can't stop this

Justice never sleeps, they can't kill righteous memories

Too many have died by phantom menaces
disguised as police officers

Daily the so-called peace officers can
kill unarmed ghetto youths

But society labels ghetto youths the menaces?!

It's too Much

Hard to maintain nature in a superficial world

When ghoulish thoughts appear as Art

The psychological immune system becomes compromised.

Tearing around the clock voices out of tune

Verbal shifty imaginations running wild in narrow spaces

Antennas are bent or broken from Circassian
scabies growing on the cranium

Therefore, receptors can't receive
anymore reduced to baldness

Synthetic addictions draining the melanin from faces

Congested case overcrowds, where the poor
is penalized for being desperate

No time to meditate

The collective focus is on appeasing the instincts

Separated from the whole, immured by the
five senses give pecuniary architects the power
to regulate and market destructive behavior

Treating the poor as stimulus packages

Who rejuvenates the Reflectors

Bajah Oginga Langley

The poor processors of vitamin D.

The interceptors of Rhythm robbed Soul Train

Got on board dissected and abstracted the Rhythm

The only way they could energize and bring to life

A ream of deplorable simulated creations.

It

Excited… It uncoils creeping up the spine

Temperature in the biological rises

Central nervous system tingles

Like a serpent, It slithers activating the senses

The sensation provides a warm and smooth feeling

It moves past the abdomen

Penetrates the heart vibrating the chakras
controlling the blood's circulator

Blood rushes flooding the procreative complementary organs

Moving up further It enters the faculty of vision the pineal gland

The transitory eyes close and the Infinite Eye opens

It reaches its peak

Its wings unsheathe creating a massive explosion

Millions of atoms are released

Zigzagging to its destination, but only one cell survives

No life can arrive without It

It could be your greatest Ally

Or It will be your greatest Adversary

Bajah Oginga Langley

The Subtle One

Held captive by some doppelganger force

Regulated by a subtle puppeteer…

It unseen hand the Invisible Man

Plucking my soul like some congenetic fiber
connected to the astral realm

Stardust thrown into my eyes fettered by deception

Subjected me to years of its application of nonsense

The Invisible Force forgot its eclectic nature and became the
Sandman using my dreams as a playground

Capitulation to this complication fossilized my freedom

Trapping my subconscious like a fly in a web enticed
by crystal-like sounds and images

Chasing objective Ideals twisted my mind into an
unusual period of projected psychosis

Now, the fiyah that sparked life has become glacier-like

But still, having enough flare to clench my fist
in this abyss of subjective mirages

However, suddenly unfrozen and struck by awe discovering the
illustrious reflection of me holding a crown and a key

Able to set free my faculties proving that…

The doppelganger is, no one but me!!!

Intuition

She sashayed into the room with power
exuding from her essence

Immediately, she commanded my attention without makeup or
any other accessories of masked pretension

Instantly filled with acuity for her realizing she was a
Boss on the hunt to possess a man who could
add more light to her lighthouse

Staring as she moved like a quiet storm yet stepping gracefully

A tsunami of feelings elevated me with
confidence to accept her challenge

There could be no pretense in order to inherit her

Only the unadulterated appealed to her, while machismo men
appearing overconfident were disregarded

Sensing she was a Reckoning attracted to natural Instinct…
not some fraudulent pondering trying to lure her with a few
seconds of unproductive conversation

Nah, she was much too intelligent and spiritual

Deep in the Roots and wasn't just satisfied
with things mundane and physical

Evoking her must be beyond the corporeal ways of searching

Summoning her, a man has to be like a sun
able to shower her with edification

Bajah Oginga Langley

A man who brightens her "essential mirror" indoors as well as
without without light never descending

Just relying on tangible senses doesn't
stimulate her atmosphere

Her search was for an Astral Cosmopolitan in the present
that much becomes clear as a virgin river

To the finite, she was a Hidden Figure over-looked
due to her organic appearance

As she got closer, I could feel her superlative Aura
flooding the whole room, allowing my soul to start absorbing
her energy even from a distance

On the edge of my seat, it felt like I was about to be elected
and was the prominent candidate selected
to govern her radiant Providence

Her brilliance emitted from the sparkle in
her eyes with her head

Wrapped up in a multicolored Turban pointing to her
sophistication, but never forgetting how to
keep the balance with the urban

A pure Impression of Eden without arrogance nor
constricted, but flexible, knowing her worth shield her from
subterfuges escaping the snares of the miserable…

Ah, she is an Angelic Principle, a Mobile Garden,
a benevolent depiction of nature

The Domesticated Escape

Kidnapped even though I put a strong resistance

Too rebellious, no cooperation with bestializing

So I'm forced to run in a sensual place trying to escape the
house built on sand

Too many are caught tamed, trained, domesticated like Angus
cattle forced to adapt to the house gone with the wind

Captured, no matter, I plot and escape again

Take a deep breath, exhale and sprint again

I hear dogs

Hard to see through the fog

I stumble upon a graveyard rest a bit, and sprint again

Still, I hear the hounds getting closer

But with determination I run harder, feeling confident until…

I trip and fall into a swamp full of water moccasins

The air grows colder, but I am full of assurance and discipline

Swimming harder…

I reach fertile ground without getting bitten

Journeying further…

Bajah Oginga Langley

I can still hear dogs yelping a sign they are getting nearer

All I got on is a potato sack to cover my
loins that's now damped

No shirt, no shoes, no food…I reek of the swamp

No map to guide me through the weltered thicket of morbidity

Yet, justice smiles on me

Down comes the rain to conceal my scent

A hand reaches out

I smile before I pass out

The dogs barking fades away as I drift away from exhaustion

90 years bondaged to carnality…

But, I awake on the other side of Jordan

I think I made it!

Am I really finally un-domesticated?!

Relieved, but wait!

I hear a scruffy voice say…

Gal, whar did dis here nigra come from?!

The Election of Jack Frost

The Ice Age won the election

Now, the administration of the Summer is forced into exile

No wonder why the country is so cold
pointed in Jack Frost's direction

Subordinated to a cold war and afraid…

All the other seasons have submitted and
teamed up with the winter

Conspiring to destroy the summer

Jack Frost's general Lee's presidency finally came to fruition

The battle: Who will be in control of Light or darkness

The hot or the cold?

The Tropical environment of the frozen level?

The North Pole won the election and Jack Frost is the president

Elected by a democracy that thrives in frigid temperature

The administration of the nippy

Always vying to be the only season relevant

Competition to bridle the heat of the soul

Brown eyes, broad nose, and bronze skin…

Bajah Oginga Langley

The energetic model now below zero

Under control by the cold is the
advertised model for all seasons

People of the sun

Frozen from neglecting to burn the soul's coal

Surrendering to a governmental blizzard

Neutralizing the heat within the soul empowers the Ice Age

Submission entrapped the vortex of heat in a galactic snowball

Can't beat 'em might as well join 'em"

Formed an alliance with winter selling their Black oil cheap

Giving up their repellent against the winter to be accepted
and begging for a little place in the snow

But only paid the dark experience of physical and material
sensation quick stimulations created by artificial pharmaceutical

Jack Frost's mission…

To acerbate any souls vulnerable to the elements of the cold

Jack Frost knows….

If the winter lingers too long around the astral body

Melanin won't absorb enough heat to produce energy

Instead, the soul will become an ice-house

Yet the absorption of heat revives the Soul
when Black circulates energy

Each time heat radiates

The Prison Philosopher

Life has arisen in its Divine Presence

Other than that

Mutations in the present dominate in a
place extremely cold and foggy,

Where heat doesn't circulate well

Meaning, Jack Frost had the Soul in its palm-

The power of Mr. Freeze

A freak of nature, but possesses enough
charms to do harm to

Suspension of the Soul is the absence of Light

Chilly temperature is activated

Then winter takes control of the distribution of Heat

Heat, the rejuvenation of life and its evolution

Heat the Art and Beat of the heart and its creative expression

Heat can sunburn winter's cronyism

So all the seasons could experience Intensity

Heat is the balance that challenges and
melts snowstorm avalanches

Yet, Jack Frost election overpowered all the seasons

Implementing a policy causing Frigidaire
mutations in all seasons…

Bajah Oginga Langley

Spring, summer, and Fall was frostbitten

No equality under Jack Frost's jurisdiction

Envious because he knows the winter
isn't the original providential

Source of Radiancy

Ping – Pongs

So, we aren't against you…

We are against your system of vampirism

Speaking truth to power is our Declaration

We can't keep supporting deception

Voting to maintain either a higher or lesser evil

Evil is evil, no matter how it's articulated

How long must we be used by political percussionists-

In a civil war, mentality between the south and the north?!

We are still captive exploited nouns converted to adjectives

Born into a system where we don't write our own narratives

How could we when we can't read, nor write in English?

Thus, our lives are reductions of being supporting actors or
props never choosing our own roles to play

Not knowing our true roles to showcase

Lead us to be objectively possessed by foreign subjective
suggestions who feed off our souls…

This is why the world appears too cold to us

Let liberals say, be optimistic

Bajah Oginga Langley

Even though we live in a country where the cops can
murder us on a Reality show while the courts tell us not to be
pessimistic…reform Is coming after the election?!

Then we wake up to see or hear another one
of us murdered by their guns or chokeholds?!

When will it stop?!

Liberal and conservatives tricked the world into believing
that the United States is a United nation….

However, we are 13% of the population

But 38.6% of us are warehoused in Americka's prisons–

Mostly for minor offenses

Oppression against US

Continues to be relentless,
no matter who sits in the Oval Office.

Nonsense

Poor folks stay going through a lot of unnecessary
manipulatory events no collective power debating politics

What's the point when the poor districts aren't considered
relevant geopolitical events until their votes are needed?

Nevertheless, poor people are the consumers
who keeps the economy turning

Bajah Oginga Langley

Wise Up!

Prison is a place where so-called Thugs end up in retirement

However, you still have to pay taxes,
but minus a pension in the future

And forget about your social being secured because they say

Prisoners are not citizens in Amerika

Your people can't even collect insurance,
if God forbid, you should die in prison

The state government gets the insurance money

Divide 3/5's of the profits with the Federal government

Yeah, thanks to our ignorance and not being independent

Be assured though…

Not every prisoner accepts the prison's
architecture of dependency

No way!

For there's a small faction striving for
redemption and Emancipation

With the guidance repelling the psychological
madness running wild in

The prison subculture

The struggle…Trying hard not to be a
victim like the dastard offenders

The Prison Philosopher

Those unrehabilitated miscreants being laughed at

From the comedy, they display every second
on prison's candid cameras

I'm talking about those effeminate inmates

The court's proscribed dependents
content in a misfitted environment

Flowing through the prison's atmosphere is incompetence

Neo-religion was born when they
introduced the 13th amendment

the law labeling prisoners forever slaves in Amerika

After being convicted

Hardly anyone is exempt from being influenced
by prison's asinine faculties

Even when separating yourself from the
prison's method of dystopia

Insanity still has the power to grab you
while sanity is daily crucified

Sanity's frequency is better, but to no avail…

The better is always shunned and made a mockery by the
majority pushed aside for the glitter of fantasy

Those allurements for a few minutes to be a bunch of guys
engaged in rambunctious vanity

Therefore, C/O's are instructed to call Inmates gentlemen…

That's right, gentlemen!

Bajah Oginga Langley

Reincarnated negro sambos still trying to
impress descendants of colonizers?..

Yahsuh boss…Iz a nigga, a good nigga, in chorus they sing

But, a tablespoon of molasses and a biscuit

Are the only payments a nigga gets for being a good nigga

Occasionally, a good nigga gets the chance to
spit watermelon seeds on the 4th of July

Independence for former colonizers and their descendants

But slaves feel the need to participate in the festivities
of their own enslavement (imprisonment)?!

The whole world is watching in disgust and humor, you fools!

The Square

The modern-day penal system

The ultimate disengagement from life

Entangled by earthworm impressions

Reflections of intellectual regression

Where mental health try to survive off good memories
however, with no new experiences, life is fading away

The environment is designed to affect the conscience
with worthless social asphyxiations

In order to feel alive today

You have to figure out a way to be reborn each day

Go to sleep, wake up and find anxiety lingering over your head

Searching for the sun but its intercepted by depression

Nature equipped us with Halos

But once convicted, you're blotted out from the Book of Life

Imprisoned rewired and then placed in a garden of impassivity

Thought we were freed in 1863
but our bloodline never left the prison

From generation to generation we live and die in prison

Never hearing the freedom song, we reincarnate in prison

Bajah Oginga Langley

Crimination is the realm of demoralization

A perimeter of contorted nightmares turning suns into flares

Who becomes no more than a spark

Whose bushes are planted here except their
beauty is mental hypomanic horns

Poison ivies getting paid to feed off emotions
get injected and infected by their psychological venom

Your brain cells transform into a tombstone

After count time you come out a walking dead
roaming around in a Dormitory

Still alive amongst the slumbers

Psychopathic darts are aimed at your head

Until your mind and outside resources are cut off

And you submit to wearing sackcloth

Staying awake, they try to convince you
that staying awoke is madness

Make you doubt reality, make you think you lost your family

Trapped in a square bouncing you around from point to point

Dejected and exhausted, you forget how to do simple math

Incarceration, where time is a furnace turned up to the maximum

Time here is a sociocultural crematorium burning
up the last remnants of humanity

Here in the square lies are the most powerful

The Prison Philosopher

Ingratiates for the system are empowered
to spread asperity like bacteria

This is the ascension of factitious clouds blocking life's smiles

Freedom is Federal, the slaves are states in a period of desertion

Prisoners are Revolutionist, inmates are penological stories

The Rehabilitated comprehend the cause
the offenders stay incarcerate

By the effects of crime

So tell me…Who are the real criminals…those who architect the
square or those who build the square?

Bajah Oginga Langley

Madness and Sadness

The Truth is… existing positive around so many bipolar
characters is out of the question

Too many strains of different personalities caught up in
deceptive performances disregarding their essence of nature.

Compacted psychodynamics acting out preludes to madness

Worshipping outdated modes of theology in the 21st century

No advances in their modes of reasoning

Because it's magnified by madness

Stuck in a fabricated unprincipled religion ending up in sadness

Due to mental dimness progression is non-existent

Preponderance of backwardness encapsulate
them into a social distance

No heartfelt songs are sung in this place

Only the melodies of aggression

In a Jurassic Park for human dinosaurs used as
paychecks and, penal amusements

Mental regressive congestion prevents you from
seeing the stars…clouds of sadness

Hard times when you are living in a lie of foolishness

Good times depleted from mass sullenness

I hate it!

The Prison Philosopher

All the madness and sadness.

On top of that…

Why does the media paints gloomy pictures of social
irrationality, knowing most have blind eyes
and can't understand madness?

The media mostly is a contortion of reality

And as a people, we are stuck in a limbo
of madness and sadness

We use to build temples giving birth to
neonatal spiritual enhancements

Now they call us mental defects with arrogance

Playing games in their system like saying we are equal,
but separated…they're real hilarious

I've learned you can't trust a people that's full

Who turn people into sheep just to shave their wool

When dogs bark…

They see zombified people in captivity roaming lightheaded,

Walking around giddy cause they lost their memory

Man, every freakin' day some mother has to attend
a funeral from the feeling of sadness

Pleading to God to resurrect her son who
died before he was born

Bajah Oginga Langley

Because he was killed by madness

Another Branch tore from the Tree of Life

Or some sent to prison to swing from a
Tree for Life of madness and sadness

This can't be right, or is it?!

But the truth is… it's hard being positive
in the underprivileged world

No comfort for the weary where the future looks dreary

Because present conditions are weak
backpacking madness and sadness

Incubated in a cloned system molded us
with irrational covetousness

Then snatched out the womb, naked to madness

The "projects" turned us into buffoons of craziness

Public schools introduced our minds to the English harpoons

Since then, inferior status

Ruled by a government of wizardly making
their women appear classy

Lusting after a paled emaciated physique
enticing us to eat madness

Along came sadness, once our eyes were brainwashed

Only wanting her portal of low energy

Put snowfall in our streets for the young to digest

The Prison Philosopher

That cold climate scoring each time a Black child is born poor

Trying to get rich selling narcotics

The bald eagle gets the energy and screech with achievement

I can't take it anymore….

The system of the unscrupulous is a trip of madness,

Journey of Predatorial ways leading to sadness

Blood on the conductors of madness and sadness hands

And, they don't feel a guilty conscience

Ain't that some profane brashness?!

But the Truth is… Consciousness is dead in the 21st century

However, I refuse to speak through thin lips…

Nah, I will never choose that!

Bajah Oginga Langley

Serious Business

It's serious business when you are a Revolutionary

Steady being watched, criticized and plotted against by
masquerader agents and their flunkies

The business is serious…

Displaying a revolutionary performance

Many have died trying to eradicate racism,
levels of exploitive extreme

Materialism instant synthetic simulation…

The things fueling Kapitalism

Kapitalism… you can have it all, rushes of instant success

Instant fame, instant glory, and instant power

As long as you suck on Kapitalism's breasts

Life is a party…

The philosophy and religion of the west

But for the Revolutionary that can understand
the trinkets of stress…

Fast living incites the imagination to fall victim
to instant entrapments of duress

Instant materialism camouflaged as
accelerated abundant satisfaction

Kapitalism marauding treats to trick, produce,

The Prison Philosopher

and reduplicate its redundant illusion of pretend wealth

Bewitched by Kapitalism a legion is created

Loyal followers become capitalist cult followers

But, end up humans treated as stocks traded around the clock

Sacrificial flocks dying young and slavish

Then, placed in caskets preserved to
Someday refuel materialism

When Kapitalism loses its energy

Kapitalism cannot replenish itself

Unless materialism can convert human beings into energy

Instant gratification…

A labyrinth for those who are born to worship unicorns

And upside-down five-pointed stars with horns
created by fornicated architects seeking to dismantle
and stop Revolutionary Regiments

It's serious Business and can be somber…
for the Revolutionist!

Bajah Oginga Langley

False Impression is Loved

Lies and lying happens to be a subtle assault on life

Like a drug, lies are intoxicating for a brief moment

Lies and lying are the ultimate fascinating,
captivating, stimulating fiction

Yet, ends up being a downer

Many are called, but a few are chosen to be Truth

But in a world of lies Truth is abnormal and the
pretenders are the accepted norm

Reality is scoffed at and ostracized

Lies are the images and lying is the sounds many
choose to look at, listen to, and embrace

Truth last longer, but not the chosen healing interface

Lies is the quick fixes the pretender's fiend
for to define their existence

The pretenders keep lying and creating lies to
stop Truth from existing…

A ploy to keep infecting reality with its false persona

Duration

There was a Time when "Emancipation" was the motivation

There was a time when "Black Power" was the Inspiration

Then there was a Time when "Fight the Power"
birthed an uplifting 20th century Expression,
a applicable impressionistic slogan

But, in the Twenty-first century, time slid down the ladder into
the king dumb of drunkards and dullards…

Disturbed generation with inherited mental scars
grounded in a petri dish screaming…

It's Time for racism to end!

It's Time for police brutality to end!

It's Time for collective poverty to end!

It's Time for Black Folks to win!

But, how do you win in a time of the Pretends
camouflaged as your people?

How can you win, when time is spent running from Self?!

The saying is wrong, Time doesn't heal all things

Because time is present and past events and
experiences created and controlled by interpreters,
Intermediaries, and Interlopers

Comprehending experiences in current moments

Bajah Oginga Langley

heals unwholesome conditions

Comprehension creates time, harness time, and tames time

Where victory is guaranteed for the living

However, structured by Time is the Bearer of gloomy
portends for collective cogenerations in the past, and in
the present with a stuporous future

Subjective Pillagers

Subjective pillagers thrive off lust, greed, fear,
envy, hate, and jealousy

Thirsting for life, but weighed down by mortality

Born and raised to war

Keeping the tradition of lawlessness as a medium
to gain power from nightmares

Each nightmare is a reincarnated evil encore

Unable to carve up Dark Matter when it is
separated from their roots

Opening up the door where generational extortions can use
duality to liquidate and siphon melanin

Transforming into objective photographers

Taking pictures of souls to extract souls from their film

Traveling like chaffs in the wind

Searching for those embedded with the Shine

Those souls who haven't discovered the
Infinite expansion within…

Becomes the unawakened getting their steam slurped up

Until they join the congregation of the declined

Finding their minds confined to sleep

Bajah Oginga Langley

Where lust, greed, fear, envy, hate, and jealousy
are fed to the subjective goblins

This is the Invasion of elfin creatures raiding sleep…

to conquer the abstract Pantheons concealed
in the subjective realm

One Colour

Elysium on Earth when all Colours come together and
form one colour – blinded Federation…

Or Dystopia on Earth if the colours remain distant bickering
about what colour had the right to rule and be highlighted

Here's wisdom… Every Colour in Nature vibrates in
Unison under the blue sky and take nourishments
from the depths of the blue seas

Nature holds no belief, no impartiality until man caused the
separation of nature's spectrum to appear as a dual reality

Disconnected from nature, man's mind became a grief
projection painted on a blank screen of emptiness

Using a pseudo-science diluted Colour trying
to erase traces of pigmentation

Hoping to use melanin as a source to create
a suggested illusionary imagination

A meaningless division became a reality amongst the colours
suppressing the beauty amongst one another

Still, the sun shines whether the sky is blue or gray…

So why all the hate, envy, and xenophobia?!

Why can't all the Colours no longer relate…

When all Colours originated from One Hue
not from a blank canvas!

Bajah Oginga Langley

Revelations

Imagine waking up in a cold sweat from the
threats of being terminated

A New World order, so long, the Illuminati have waited

The Matrix has risen under the pretense of Democracy

Fiction became the reality, giving birth to a New Testament

A New Pope, a New President

Revelations speak of a whore with a cup

Many nations drink her intoxicants

Clash of the religions, war on the horizon

Star wars new god new currency is the face of
Steve Jobs and Ronald Reagan

Each day gets worst and millions suffer from
hunger games growing fangs

Father against sons and mother against daughters
from technocrats encodings

Immigrants breaking through the border

Who fall victim to hypnotism imperialism and fascism

Now the masses recognize they aren't equal crying out for the
constitution to be applied to them too…

But while they partied their constitutional rights
was snatched before their eyes

The Prison Philosopher

Never seen it coming even though a virus
showed up with a warning

Troops were dispatched as they partied to
gather a mass incarceration

Oblivion seeps in traumatized Human Beings stop believing in
a God except for the ones created by unseen hands

A new 'band of terror' appears from nowhere

A 21st century nightmare declares a reign in this area

Crucifixes…Preacher's words turn into nitroglycerin

A lot of pandemonium

Sunday mornings many wake up to see cross burnings

More denying but can't find no shelter

Why? Because no one believed a helter
skelter could happen in Amerika

Under the rule of terror, mothers are pregnant with clones
asbestos and lead in their bones

The Fetuses in the womb indoctrinated to be
fodder in the Twilight Zone

The Mark of The beast, a mental cancer
feasting on human minds like meat

Trying to breathe in poverty, instead finding misery

Democracy pisses on the world and defecating anarchy

The dark becomes the sun and the sun becomes the dark…

Bajah Oginga Langley

Waking up in a cold sweat realizing so many have no
hearts in an era of destituted conditioning

Graven Images

Living licentious clouds the eye

Stuck in a callous mental complexion explains why
so many die young and desolate

Unconsciousness the baptism of Hell

A tunnel vision of aberration vampires rule
a congregation of the dead

The place where madness bounces back
and forth in your head

A place where optical miseducation kneels
you before you can walk

A sordid intuition doesn't allow you to make the right decisions

Worth billions, but end up buried in a prison's vault tortured
by deranged confessions screamin'

For some type of deliverance hoping respite finds you
in a desensitized environment

Trapped in a place where project experiments drain
your energy subtracting the good from your recollection
putting your consciousness to sleep

It's either wake up or be reduced to criminal activity awakening
to see guns drawn from being a pawn in the game

In a split second bleeding to death on somebody's lawn
with a twisted face from the pain

But no one helps you because they see your
fangs spooked by your graven image

Weakness

Lost and trapped in a gray T-shirt and gray pliant pants trying to
carry depression, anxiety, and regrets with only three pockets

Not forgetting forced to walk in crippling shoes
deforming my path each step I take

The results of mistakes made for being a slave to
the lower self jurisdiction

The lower self jurisdiction…The realm for
distorted consciousness

The realm leading the subconscious to an addictive
materialized low valued substance

Never going beyond the basic needs of securing food, clothing,
and shelter gorilla glued me to a physical frequence

Steady being attacked by manic activities, like lust and greed

So now I stand at the crossroads of the mundane and
subatomic particles trying to decide which way leads to the
pinnacle where the free congregates, the sphere where Mr. Hyde
dies and everyone there related seeing with one eye

Plus, eternal, because time has dismounted the mind…

However, not liberated yet, for now, I still reside where the red,
white, and blue fly high and dominates a state where a beginning
has an end, a ghostly fate reflecting a lower self jurisdiction

Bajah Oginga Langley

Immunity

You pulled me over because of the Colour of my skin

Using a pretense to check to see if I have a license?!

See Black or Brown, and automatically you see criminal

Propagandized to hunt me down and shoot me like an animal

Feeling empowered by your badge being armed
and trained to be a Gestapo

Mr. Officer, I'm just trying to get home,
remain calm…was I speeding?

My hands are on the steering wheel, see I don't
want no trouble…I am complying

I see your hand on your gun…thinking about moving
up the ranks a hero Mr. Officer?!

Rights to brag to your cronies Mr. Officer?!

But is there really honor in killing an unarmed
Black or Brown person Mr. Officer?!

Mr. Officer, please don't shoot…I am unarmed and not resisting

Your reply, "I was reaching for a gun,
therefore, precautions was to shoot…

I carry a badge protecting me from getting
indicted for blatant cold-blooded murder…

I belong to a Force that allows me to type
up a report to a grand jury…

The Prison Philosopher

Our kind always fits the descriptions of
suspects wanted for theft and murder…

My shield is all it takes to keep me guiltless never
charged with killing the Life of Black Matter!"

You stopped me, because of the Colour of my skin, the texture
of my hair, and the color I am wearing?!

You see solid colors and you think I am a gang banger?

Stop…Freeze and put your hands up, you shout!

I put my hands up and then you squeeze the
trigger on your Glock 40 anyway

Thinking the Rico Law applies to all Ghetto children who don't
fit the facial description of white Amerika…

Thinking you have the authority to shoot me in the
streets without warning, nor regret…

Type up a report to the grand jury that you
thought I had a weapon and you felt threatened,
because I had a hoody on my head?!

Bajah Oginga Langley

Before you squeeze that Trigger

So this is what it comes to…

You pointing a gun in my face?!

But I ain't afraid, though

See, I'm looking you dead in the eye

And yeah, I can see the hate

However, before you squeeze that trigger

Let me explain to you what will happen…

Squeeze the trigger and you will be branded a nigger

And an enemy of the race

Almost like a viper

Your own kind will run from you upon sight

And from the fright alone

Your own people will want to see you go to prison

Your homies will be rapacious to take your place

Compete to sex your girl and take over your paper route

The envy will finally have its day to shine

In time your name will vanish like you are already in the grave

Your son will cry until your memory becomes dust in his eyes

The Prison Philosopher

Your daughter will grow up to call another man daddy

And when you call home

She will repeat Jody's name gladly

And all you'll be able to do is get madder

Your blood will boil and your heart will flutter

All because of a quick dose of hate

Made you squeeze that trigger…

Pow!

Game over!

Bajah Oginga Langley

K2 Induction

Eyes dispassionately red and depending on the type,
sometimes, cowardly yellow (Tunchi)

The psychoactive substance release
dopamine once I inhale (Tunchi)

Triggering distorted images lodged in
my subconscious (Tunchi)

No longer conscious of what's in front,
Behind, and around me (Tunchi)

Becoming a narrative for another episode of
the Walking Dead (Tunchi)

A synthetic chemical invasion wreaking havoc on
my central nervous system (Tunchi)

Lost in space…the aging process accelerates
from the look on my face (Tunchi)

About to be a statistic, one more Imbecile
hooked on the casket high (Tunchi)

Sometimes I feel like I can fly (Tunchi)

Sometimes I feel like I am paralyzed (Tunchi)

Sometimes I feel like I'm goin' ta die (Tunchi)

Sometimes, I think I am seeing God (Tunchi)

Don't want to eat, bathe, or sleep (Tunchi)

Reduced to having an irregular heartbeat,
but…I still want to smoke… (Tunchi)

Judas Takes Over

Guarded by the retarded…

Life moves at a snail's pace walking around
with the lost and broken-hearted

Because Judas detained the mind and captured the
faculty of reasoning shackled to a fleshy detention
arrested the heart's emotional circulation

Judas dethroned Love

So Judas established a law, a creed

Providing the body with obscenities and
charging taxes to breathe air

Under this rule, any thoughts of purity are
sought out and drowned

No more uplifting thoughts
desensitized, the heart grows weaker

In debilitation, Judas grows in power and stature

Forcing the other faculties to either accept
Judas's thirty pieces of deicide and makes cupidity
your God, or be thrown in the den of aversion

Going further…

Judas hijacked the irrigation system, causing imbalance

Unable to filter the psychological pollution,
schizophrenia is born

Bajah Oginga Langley

No Exodus for the captured sinking in Juda's doldrum sinkholes

No!

As long as the denatured keeps supporting Judas's biological,
psychological, and economical betrayal.

Pledging to the Ancient of Days

Entering the Gates of Addis Ababa saluting the Lion of Judah

Celebrating the Life of Selassie I Pledge to
honor the Life Restoring Ancestor

Life in a Day is now longer since the arrival of the King of Kings

Foreign occupation flees from Righteous Judgement

The Springs of RASTAFARI echoes from
Players on Instruments

Red, Gold, and Green elevated to Crown the Earth

Signaling the Wealth of the Universe has
been distributed upon Haile I Selassie is birth to all
the sons and Dowtas of the Sun…July 23rd

Many around the world, at home and scattered
abroad hear the voices of the Angels sing
a Child King was born unto InI

Love comes out of exile with a smile
meaning the Nile is purified

Sons and Dawtas of the Sun are baptized

Lies loses its grip when HIS Majesty utters Fiyah from HIS lips

JAH RASTAFARI…The Seven Seals open

The Book of Life begins to demystify

Babylon falls to its knees in acknowledgement

Bajah Oginga Langley

Selassie, I unshackle the Sons of Dawtas held in captivity

RASTAFARI the Ancient of Days restored in memory

334th Negus this man was born there to continue the Abyssinian Independence and Afrikan diaspora redemption

Here and There FAR-I everywhere

Gives Ises Satta Massagona

JAH RASTAFARI… HAILE I SELASSIE I

Uhuru SaSa Everywhere!

Part Three

The Analytical Prisoner:

Meditations
& Social Warnings

Chapter One: The Mind

1. Investing in your mind is the best investment you can make.

2. Imagine better, and you will become better at doing better.

3. Knowledge stops and becomes irrelevant when your mind falls within the grips of idle thinking.

4. When under the duress of oppression, revolutionize your mind with positive impression and the manacles of psychological oppression will release your psyche.

5. It's never cool to be stupid. Stupidity is the epitome and cause of mental sicknesses.

6. An enslaved mind will keep love suppressed and make love appear as a desolated emotion.

7. Your brain is the greatest organ in your body. However, the brain shrinks when your mind doesn't think right.

8. God is an Ultimate Force in your mind, your Personal Creator that connects you to the Image, Likeness, and Force of the Omnipresent creator.

9. Good and bad thoughts are subtle images and messages constantly struggling for governance over the mind by producing impressionistic thought suggestions. Both, though impressions and suggestions (good and bad), are constantly vying to find outlets for expressing itself through the mind's faculty. This is Armageddon, the battle of the expression of thoughts where your mind is the battleground.

10. One bright Idea can add years and productivity to your life, while one bad idea can end it quickly.

11. Poverty and its appearance are a state of mind. Poverty exists when a person perceives themselves to be poor. This mental state actually causes the thinker to become the definition of poverty.

12. The mind contains the complete perfections of life, which denaturation tries to destroy. Once the mind can no longer conceive, envision, receive, contain, retain, or produce life conceptions, it becomes no more than a wasteland.

13. Anyone easily manipulated can be controlled. Once a person is suited to be controlled, their mind no longer belongs to them, but the manipulator.

14. When a person lives in the shadows of hate their mind becomes a breeding ground for self-destruction.

15. The ingenuity of the mind is that the mind is capable of producing affluent thoughts. Producing and consuming the right psychological nutrients keeps you from the path of the imbecile, the road that leads to deplorable situations.

16. Criminals are not born criminals. Criminals are carefully made and molded by the criminal-minded influencers who have control over the psychosocial and socioeconomic imagination medium.

17. Positive words are positive thinking in motion. However, disparaging words are insipid thoughts in action that cannot uplift, add vigor and creativity to life.

18. Any condition can be changed with the right concept, along with having an imagining scope that prevails over mere wishful thinking.

19. If the mind is bombarded with based gross desires, the mind produces endless torments and agitation bounding the mind to the lower sphere of animalism the way the body rules over the mind.

20. The mind is like some elite university…a school for abstract revelations.

21. Keeping your mind furbished and garnished with a universal panoramic mindset allows you to create works worthy of emulation.

22. Learning and practicing what's right free your conscience, which blocks guilt and depression from leading you into dementia.

23. A person's reality is shaped and fashioned by the thoughts they feed into the womb of their mind.

24. True liberation begins once you begin to filter your mind from all the falsehood and myopic ideas placed there since birth.

25. You become what your mind consumes and processes.

26. Your mind is your property used to procure and secure your intellectual.

27. A strong mind creates and shapes a robust body.

28. Struggle is a mental exercise, a workout teaching life's strengths, and life's weaknesses.

29. You live how you think and think how you live.

30. Ideas have to turn into action in order to have any meaning and purpose.

31. What the mind can truly see, it will feel. And, what the mind can truly feel, it will see.

32. If the mind is corrupt, it will yield nothing but a state of mourning.

33. Do not let negativity have a voice within your mind, or a negativity magnetic frequency going wherever you go.

34. A person who doesn't like to think for themselves will condemn, dispute, and scorn, everything others say.

35. Let mirages train your mind and you will forget what's real and how to be real.

36. Like white blood cells, positive thinking will search, find, and destroy psychological parasites.

37. Virtue assassinates evil, while the ignoramus shields evil.

38. Demons are distorted thoughts and feelings that torture the mind.

39. When you train the mind to think introspectively, the mind will learn how to think, see, and understand at will.

40. If your mind creates ugly impressions, your whole outlook will be surrounded by ugliness.

Chapter Two: Meditation

1. Knowledge is a Universal Omnipresent Being and can be overstood by daily reflections on Self, one's social interactions, and one's environment.

2. The oppressed, gives the oppressors more power than they deserve by accepting oppression. Oppression is an idea becoming a reality once the oppressed accept oppression as a reality convinced they are powerless to defeat it. Destroy the idea of oppression and the oppressed can obliterate what appears to be an oppressive existence.

3. Experience makes you grow wiser and more skillful. However, repetitive experience blocks creativity, slows down productivity, and keeps you from evolving.

4. If you are blind, eat carrots! If you are educated, don't be a parrot!

5 Good memories curtail and dissolve sadness.

6. The more energetic power you can muster up and possess, the more creative you will be in this world.

7. Each good thing you do unselfishly, no matter how small or big, does something to better you, this world, and the people around you. Each kind act you imparted to someone has a boomeranging effect.

8. All people need to be stimulated with Reality, not fed a bunch of lies that keep them servile and socially impaired.

9. A will strong as iron forged with determination, overshadows and dispels doubt.

10. Nothing comes to those who wait, but stagnation.

11. Being optimistic doesn't make you naïve. Optimism sharpens your intellect and makes your imagination more potent. Therefore, it's not wise to be around, nor listen to, pessimistic people. Pessimism dulls the intellect and imagination, leaving you subjected to chronic anger, depression, and embitterment.

12. A person not afraid to ask questions, will be a person who learns the most.

13. Beauty is attitude, confidence, and the knowledge of you.

14. When you know, you know. The second you start to doubt what you know will be the second what you know will lose its power, meaning, and purpose.

15. When you learn you are preparing to teach. When you teach, you are increasing your learning.

16. What is moving is always changing. What is changing is always moving.

17. When all speak the same language, all will have the same overstanding.

18. Be committed to learning something each day and you will grow into being a creator creating, instead of just a Being in creation.

19. What makes a flower beautiful and a tree strong? Ans: Its Roots. It's the same with people. Strong Roots make a person sturdy and beautiful.

20. Knowing how to use the faculty of imagination is the first step towards being an Architect of your life. Imagination creates the blueprint, a guide that shows you how to manifest what you can imagine. Your imagination faculty is like a map. But, never get trapped in the mirages of just imaging. Do not let your imagination lead you, you should lead your imagination.

21. Environments are mental soluble conditions. By knowing your mind's insoluble nature, it will change any condition.

22. If you are promised things you desperately lack, you can and will be manipulated and controlled by the promiser.

23. Freedom is like an actor choosing what character to express.

24. Nowhere, is a place where the unconscious mind dwells until its Force is heated at the right temperature.

25. Sometimes you have to live at Random to discover your purpose and experience freedom. The way of Random is a cause that can't be programmed, nor imprisoned. Anyone or anything that can be programmed can be predicted. Anyone or anything that can be predicted can be imprisoned.

26. The best ideas come from letting your mind roam free.

27. Power is a character revealer.

28. Think back to every day you can remember, and you will find some wisdom.

29. Time is present and past events created and controlled by Interpreters, Intermediaries, and Interlopers.

30. Live moderate today, and rest salutarily tomorrow.

31. The word ugly can be defined as the lack of confidence in yourself intertwined with low self-esteem.

32. The feelings of love must be applied beyond the instinctive and sensual level in order for peace to reign supreme in your life.

33. You are never free until you are able to express yourself honestly and confidently.

34. A plethora of riches can be found in struggle. Struggle brings enlightenment, the Ultimate Jewel. But, you have to learn how to choose your struggles instead of letting someone, or something, choose a struggle for you. Then, you will find the wealth you need to get rid of the struggle and be able to move on.

35. Know what's foreign to your nature and you will never be a casualty of war.

3. Lies are the inebriation of the foolish.

37. If you are destructive you can never rest. Destruction is reciprocal to those who practice mischief.

38. Why do you keep tripping when all you have to do is tie up your shoes to keep from falling.

39. The system of racism in whatever guise makes the racist docile and retrogressive.

40. The Outer world when inverted reflects what's reality going on in our Inner World (mind).

41. You can only be tempted by the things you want, not need.

42. Create the circus, don't be in the circus.

43. Prisons are a world of nature in the reverse, in its recessive form.

44. Never be the mistakes of yesterday.

45. Art is a pathway to knowing God.

46. Comprehension is one of the keys to freedom. Comprehension is a threat to the system of bondage and human depravity. Oppressors can not profit form freedom. Therefore,

comprehension is the weapon, the method used to fight a system of ignorance.

47. Imprudence always fears Reality. Imprudence can not survive in a realm of actuality.

48. Every situation contains a moment of happiness. Seize the moment of happiness and you can use it to your advantage.

49. Truth is a strong shield an instrument for defense.

50. Running from a problem only percolates that problem. You have to solve the problem to make a problem go away.

51. When mad, laugh. When sad, laugh. When agitated, laugh. Laughter is the best therapy.

52. No one can be educated until they are ready to learn.

53. Rebelling against an unjust system is an act of Justice!

54. Life is constant movement and the circulation of energy, not the blocking of it.

55. Where there is confidence, progress will be born.

56. The creation of each human being is good, but the wrong condition can turn a good creation into a bad one if you accept it.

57. How do you know when you are asleep? Ans: When you realize you are living in a nightmare.

58. Where there are Roots, you will find seeds and discover the source of the biggest, brightest, strongest, and most fruitful long-lived Trees.

59. Living in Love is to be Human, while living instinctively is to be animalistic.

60. Happiness is free. No material wealth can compare, compete, or last, as long as it.

61. You can buy partial and temporary freedom in a country that uses its citizens as stocks and bonds. However, you will never purchase equality from your stock broker.

62. What's visualized today, creates the designs for tomorrow.

63. The most fundamental necessity in life, is Tranquility.

64. If you seek to solve the mystery of life, look no further than yourself. The Great Mystery of Life is the knowledge of yourself.

65. Life is free. Yet, in a world of the material, you have to pay a fee to maintain it!

66. The confusion in life comes from sensing that you have lost something, but cannot remember what you lost. When you can remember what you lost, you will know what to search for and will find what was lost.

67. Those that look outside, sleep, while those who look within, awaken.

68. The less people know, the louder they are. Ignorance lives and tries to hide itself in the noise.

69. The hardest thing to do is what's right. The second hardest thing is living with your conscience when you don't do what's right.

70. Money and ideas are one and the same. In reality, money is no more than some abstract idea turned into currency.

71. The poor are those who do not know how to extract rich ideas from their minds. The rich are opportunist who knows the mind is a money factory that can produce rich ideas to be used as

currency where creative ideas can be exploited, marketed, and sold.

72. A happy customer is like a drunken customer, they will always keep spending money.

73. Everyone has wealth buried deep within them. There's a pricey treasure submerged within everyone. If you are poor, it's only because you have yet to discover and excavate your hidden GEM.

74. A tutelary environment enhances your learning.

75. A person can never be free if they are doing things that have them worrying about being robbed, killed, or put into prison.

76. Focus your sight on life and what you see will glamourize your perception inspiring you to live more artistic and bountiful.

77. It's easier to see from the bottom than the top.

78. To change how something looks, change how you see.

79. You will never be able to forgive others until you are able to forgive yourself.

80. Rehabilitation focuses on the cause, while reform is used to make you forget the cause by redressing the cause and covering up the effects.

81. Every Reason carries a lesson.

82. Losing doesn't mean that you failed. You cannot fail when you lose because a loss is an experience. Experiences leads to awareness and skill. If you lose, you gain experience. Therefore, with every experience you gain, you are putting yourself in a position to win… next time.

83. What you see, hear, and feel within, is what you'll see hear and feel around you.

Chapter Three: Warnings

1. One can never be free within the system of hate. Hate gradually erodes the garden of the heart, paralyzes the health of the body, and imprisons the creativity of the soul.

2. Watch those given to folly and notice a fool never finds happiness.

3. A parent who doesn't love, nourish, nurture, teach, and protect their child (ren), is banishing their child (ren) to a cycle of victimization.

4. You either Love or hate, decide wisely. The wrong decision leads to a journey full of painful mistakes.

5. Moral weakness should never be an option unless you like living squalidly.

6. No one can buy love, but you sure can purchase misery and hell.

7. Misuse and abuse Freedom, and she'll become your worst enemy.

8. Life's a movie…a motion Picture. In your movie, either you are the Writer, Producer, Hero, Villian, a Star of a supporting actor, or a low-budget jester the whole world points at and ridicules.

9. Oppression and exploitation are two causes of discontent and revenge.

10. When life feeds off of positive energy, its frequency is enhanced and becomes more potent. However, anger, hate, licentiousness, envy, viciousness, and covetousness are low frequencies and impotence that decrease and depletes life's energy.

11. Cameras flashing, high fashion, a lot of fake smiling. The congregation of illusionists has arrived, walking on the red carpet.

12. A world of fiction is an orchestrated script written by those whose tales are derived from the crypts.

13. Living a promiscuous life is like being stranded on death row, where uncontrolled sexual desires taunt, torment, anticipates, and edge on your execution.

14. Prison in whatever form, are graveyards for the stigmatized.

15. All lies are like processed food… it's bleak and flavorless.

17. The progression for a person is to evolve morally, scientifically, politically, and economically or be pushed into social oblivion.

18. If you are a miser it's wise not to make others miserable. You can never escape misery by placing misery on others. If those around you do not feel or experience happiness, then they will not let you be happy.

19. If you can't carry your own weight, then, don't get fat.

20. When that inner voice speaks, you either get weak or revived. When that inner voice speaks, you either yield, run or follow the guide. When that inner voice speaks, you either live or die.

21. Those who move fast crashes the fastest. Moving fast, you will not see those Predatorial things above, below, or around you moving at a fast pace.

22. The deadliest enemy is the person who doesn't know their true self. They are insensate and move like an airborne plaque or like some biohazardous bomb. The unconscious person is the world's worst enemies. They are disasters waiting to happen.

23. The media's emphasis on the nature of violence, drug addictions, and promiscuity, creates criminal minds. No child is born a criminal.

24. The sadist suffers more than the person who has found humility from the experiences they have suffered. The sufferer who understands finds their humanity from the experience of suffering, while the sadist lives a cycle of repetitive torment.

25. Humanity is becoming lazy, paranoid, cartoonish, and less human, from being dependent on artificial intelligence.

26. Where there is no unity with purpose, the disorganized are preyed on and exploited by those united with a purpose.

27. The further you move away from nature, the more you become denatured and desensitized to nature.

28. We become a product of our own destruction when temporal desires turn into perverted lusting. Choose not the way of the opprobrious.

29. Mentally ingesting a lie is like drinking from a diseased cup. Verbally repeating a lie will be like having your lips break out with sores.

30. Not being able to perceive reality for what it is, entraps a person into a draconian existence.

31. The streets are mean, dangerous, unreliable, unreasonable, greedy, and viciously searching for young boys and girls to cater to their insatiable lusts.

32. If corruption bites the confused, what will manifest is discordance, a bunch of people growing fangs surviving by preying on the weak.

33. Pride, when false and exaggerated, causes many to become arrogant. Arrogancy has lead to still births for some movements

that was created to bring better social changes for the socially, politically, and economically impoverished.

34. Without the knowledge and Love for self, there can't be any love, peace, or harmony. Instead, expect chaos and disorder.

35. To be satisfied or passive with the atrocities of social, economic, and political redlining, is to be a conformist for the forces that keep the oppressed unconscious, ungodly, infantile, and disfranchised.

36. Doubt is the first stage of fear. Through doubt, fear is born and causes internal damage and the mind becomes psychosomatic for the body. Doubt creates paralysis, while fear mummifies your will.

37. The worst Inmate is a content Inmate. Life never gets any better for an Inmate.

38. Ignorance makes you a liability, but consciousness makes you an asset.

39. When you can't laugh anymore, you won't feel alive anymore.

40. By letting ignorance foment causes ignorance to multiply and shapeshift into other forms.

41. Ignorance is nothing but temporary entertainment for the conscious.

42. Face reality or face the same reality daily.

43. If you lose your identity, it'll be like losing your memory. If you lose your memory, it's easy to make you become someone you are not.

44. If you wake up and discover you are surrounded by flatterers, this means you have woken up to discover a lie.

45. When a person overstands nothing in the present, their future will be founded upon stupidity.

46. Oppressors don't live off time nor care about time. Your Energy is the only thing oppressors care about and want.

47. Procrastination and laziness don't harness time… procrastination and laziness obstruct time.

48. Demons are distorted thoughts and emotions that torture the mental.

49. The environment of imprisonment isn't designed to free the psyche, but to oppress, repress, digress, and suppress the psyche…and if it can, mortify the psyche.

50. The Will is the most powerful energy source. Your Will turns thoughts into reality, while doubt is the enemy of Will. Doubt, if it lingers too long, eventually turns into fear and fear impairs the action and motivation of Will.

51. A person who doesn't experience the present consciously, will live like a low-budget projection.

52. It may appear that deceivers are prosperous. However, in actuality, deceivers can not prosper from deception. Deception is a deceiver that agitates the mind. Deceivers gradually lead themselves to their own delusion. No one can live a peaceful and fulfilling life through deception. Deception is a deceiver that deceives the deceiver.

53. Beware of the person who can tell a lie so convincing, that the liar starts to believe the lie themselves. This kind of person, or people, are the most dangerous types.

54. Up ahead, is the road to Emancipation. To the right, is the road to depression. To the left, is the road to stupefaction. And behind, is the road to the final destination. Life is a crossroad, a path of decisions.

Credit

First and foremost, All Isis due to Haile Selassie I – JAH RASTAFARI!

Second, I acknowledge all the past and present Ancestors who stood up and stand presently fighting oppression… Those SELFLESS Beings who gave and give their lives to the struggle for the Emancipation of the oppressed.

Thirdly, to my mother, Joyce Langley, who continues to stand with me, as well as my Grandmothers and my Father, Felton Langley that had unconditional Love for me.

Fourth, to my sweet friend, Yolanda. Yolanda and I have known each other for 35 years. Yolanda, you have always kept it real and still keeping it real and keeping love directed towards me no matter what! Thank you for being a real friend and a queen on my chessboard of life.

Fifth, Dwayne Robinson, better known as Jamaica. I-Dren thank you for proving that a brotha can be trusted. I couldn't have done this without you. One Love, Star!

Sixth, to Marion Blount…Thanks for the positive feedback and the push to get this book done. And, to Paul Miller Jr. for supplying the phone calls.

Seventh, to my daughters, Black Diamond (Ferrah) and Black Pearl (Terris)…Keep being Queens that you are! I know that you both had to grow up without me being there, but you both were always loved and still loved by me. You both know that I never stop trying.

Eighth, to my four Grandchildren-Terijana, Aniyah, Ke'ziyah, and Cayden. The four of you are the legacy! Let this book inspire you to always want to know about who and what you are. Never bow to anyone or be bewitched by material things.

Ninth, to Dynasty Visionary Designs. Thanks for creating the self-publishing business that helps give prisoners like me.

And lastly, to Jabril Mizan, the author of *'So`el The Master's Servant'* book. I thank you for pointing me in the right direction. Peace to All!

The Prison Philosopher

Livication

Twenty – Nine Years Ago

Fargo!

Twenty–nine years you've been gone, or so it seems, but never were you forgotten.

Still thinking of you each day conjures up inspiration in a particular jubilant way.

Twenty–nine years you've been gone or so it seems, yet, I can still see you and feel your Go-Far Presence when the sun shines as well as when it rains.

Twenty–nine years you've been gone, or so it seems, but I can still see you riding your little red tricycle laughing and feeling free as the wind tickles your comely face.

Twenty–nine years you've been gone or so it seems, yet, I can still hear you running down the hallway up early ready to bake me a cake from your Easy-Bake Oven. Um.. umm.. delicious!

Twenty–nine years you've been gone or so it seems, and I can still see you smiling all day knowing you were Loved because you were loved making our house a home being that you were Love.

Twenty–nine years you've been gone or so it seems, but it's like you were born yesteryear, a Baby Girl born in the Tribe of the Langleys and Lees. A Day of Joy, Festivity, and Pride where both Tribes felt electrified. On June 28th, 1979, a Baby Girl was born into the world of the 70's, and that's Soul Power!

Yet, it was only to last for 13 years, then the tears poured from our dismayed eyes.

However, it took some time to realize Eternal Life was concealed in the Abstract name you inherited – Fargo, the Life that never moves slow, the Life ongoing Halo showntivotly, to continue to Glow and Flow, the Life destined to expand and Go Far, but ultimately, planning to return back to Life's Original Plan…Eternity.

Bajah Oginga Langley

Twenty-Nine years you've been gone or so it seems, but after a 18 year hiatus suddenly you reappeared dried our tears and ended our mourning through my Granddaughter's starry eyes, Terijona, Aniyah, and Keziyah. Through them, we see you rise, and we hear you speak, proving there's Resurrection and Life's is Infinity.

Fargo, your Life was never some fleeting dream. Your Life is a Service of Love straight from the Source of Omni Present Love. We know this now, so there's some Peace.

Twenty–nine years you've been gone, but your song is still a fresh melody of JAH's Precious Art and Rhythm, still Exclusive, still Essential, still Beautiful and we still Love You Fargo.

Travel on, my Beloved Sister!